P9-BUH-237

Family Traditions

This book was created as an outreach of the Heritage Builders Association—a network of families and churches committed to passing a strong heritage to the next generation. Designed to motivate and assist families as they become intentional about the heritage-passing process, these resources draw upon the collective wisdom of parents, grandparents, church leaders, and family life experts, in an effort to provide balanced, biblical parenting advice along with effective, practical tools for family living.

For more information, write, phone, or visit our Web site:
Heritage Builders Association
c/o Chariot Victor Publishing
4050 Lee Vance View
Colorado Springs, CO 80918

1-800-528-9489
www.chariotvictor.com
www.heritagebuilders.com

The Heritage Builders resources include:

The Heritage
A foundational book explaining the Heritage Builders ministry's key concepts. (Trade paper)

Family Night Tool Chest books
An Introduction to Family Nights
Basic Christian Beliefs
Christian Character Qualities
Holiday Family Nights
Money Matters Family Nights
Wisdom Life Skills

Family Fragrance
An expansion on one of the four foundational concepts of building an intentional legacy. Filled with ways to develop and create an AROMA of love in your home. (Trade paper)

Heritage Builders Curriculum
A small group adult study focusing on the importance of establishing and passing on a family spiritual heritage. (Thirteen-week curriculum)

These resources from Chariot Victor Publishing are available through your local Christian bookstore.

Family Traditions

J. Otis Ledbetter and Tim Smith

Chariot Victor Publishing
A Division of Cook Communications

Chariot Victor Publishing,
Cook Communications, Colorado Springs, Colorado 80918
Cook Communications, Paris, Ontario
Kingsway Communications, Eastbourne, England

FAMILY TRADITIONS
© 1998 by J. Otis Ledbetter and Tim Smith

All rights reserved. No part of this book may be reproduced without written permission
except for brief quotations in books and critical reviews. For information, write Chariot
Victor Publishing, 4050 Lee Vance View, Colorado Springs, CO 80918.

Editor: Marlee Alex
Cover Design: Bill Gray
Cover Illustration: Chris Ellison
Interior Design: Brenda Franklin

First Printing, 1998
Printed in the United States of America

1 2 3 4 5 6 7 8 9 10 Printing/Year 02 01 00 99 98

Unless otherwise noted Scripture quotations are from the *Holy Bible: New International
Version*® (NIV). © 1973, 1978, 1984 by International Bible Society. Used by permission of
Zondervan Publishing House. All rights reserved. Other Scripture quotations taken
from the *Holy Bible, New Living Translation* (NLT) © 1996, Tyndale House Publishers,
Wheaton, IL 60189. Used by permission; *The New King James Version* (NKJV) © 1979,
1980, 1982, Thomas Nelson, Inc., Publishers; *King James Version* (KJV).

Library of Congress Cataloging-in-Publication Data

Ledbetter, J. Otis.
   Family traditions/by J. Otis Ledbetter and Tim Smith.
      p. cm.
   Includes bibliographical references.
   ISBN 1-56476-753-1
   1. Family--Religious life.   I. Smith, Tim.   II. Title.
BV4526.2.L365   1998   98-34149
249--dc21   CIP

Table of Contents

Dedication

To my grandparents—
Carl and Marie Smith,
and Sandy and Miriam Cleveland,
in appreciation for passing on a Godly heritage.
—*Tim Smith*

To my children's grandparents—
Jack and Margaret Hover
and Lloyd and Mimi Ledbetter,
for giving Gail and me a taste for traditions that
satisfied our children's hunger.
—*J. Otis Ledbetter*

Acknowledgments

I am grateful to Leadership Network in Dallas, for their partnership with me in founding the Family Ministries Forum. It was at the Forum that I met J. Otis Ledbetter and became more acquainted with the Heritage Builders Association. I was excited to discover other people with a passion to grow strong families through the heritage concept. Some of the courageous pioneers are Randy Scott, Jim Weidmann, and Kurt Bruner. I'd like to also acknowledge the hundreds of parents who have shared their family tradition ideas, many of which are included in the book.

—*Tim Smith*

My mind turns to several people whose encouragement helped this book to completion.

To Tim Smith who has become much more than a co-author. He has become a close friend.

To my wife, Gail, whose inspiration keeps me full of admiration for her. I have become her biggest fan.

To my dear friend and secretary, Sherry, who makes sure I stay focused.

To those who know the complete value of traditions, and have kept them alive so future generations may sift through them and see their faithfulness, I owe a debt of gratitude.

And to the "laboratory animals" (also lovingly known as rug rats) Matthew, Rebecca, and Leah who lived through our experiments and actually come back to visit.

—*J. Otis Ledbetter*

Introduction

"A good man leaves an inheritance for his children's children."
Proverbs 13:22

As I (Tim) returned the rust-colored Samsonite folding chair to the hall closet, I noticed again it had my grandfather's name written under the seat: *Carl Smith.* I have lost the other three chairs in the set; this one, used when a guest joins our family for dinner, is what's left of the folding card table and chairs I inherited from my grandparents. To me, it is a treasure.

Whenever my sisters, brothers, and I visited our grandparents in their small apartment, Grandpa would pull out that folding table and chairs to make a place for us kids. Grandma would dress the table with one of her lace tablecloths, set it with her finest silver, china, and crystal: small bowls for pickles—sweet and dill, salt and pepper in fancy shakers, a heavy cutglass water pitcher, and a vase filled with flowers (usually pansies from her tiny garden). It didn't matter that the table was set for children—and that china breaks easily. We were her *grand*children, and we were special.

Dinner always lived up to our highest expectations. Roast beef, mashed potatoes, carrots, tossed salad, fresh-baked rolls with homemade jam, real butter, and a fresh apple pie were common fair. But what made us feel loved wasn't the food. It was the focus. We kids never felt left out or ignored. We had everything at the kids' table that the adults had at the big table, and sometimes more. Before any of us could sneak a bite, Grandpa asked the blessing and thanked God for His provision. The topic of God and spirituality was woven into "please pass the berry jam" and "want some more 'gherkins'?" After dinner, the folding table would be cleared, the tablecloth removed, and Scrabble or Chinese checkers set up.

My grandparents, who didn't have a TV, VCR, or computer, spent hours playing with us. They hadn't much money, but they had time. They knew the value of passing on *legacy.* They started with what they had, not with what they *wished* they had. As retired missionaries, many years in ministry, most of their prime was spent working in small churches, and later, with Child Evangelism Fellowship, introducing hundreds of children to Jesus. The folding table was also used plenty to prepare mailings, curriculum for Bible clubs, and crafts for children.

Food. Fun. Conversation. Commitment to service. All this occurred around my grandparents' folding table. From them I learned that I was a person of worth, had gifts and abilities to invest, and should use them to benefit others. Their example was my impetus for going into the ministry, particularly with children and youth. Grandpa had no idea what an investment he was making at Sears when he purchased the table set for twenty dollars. He passed on a valuable inheritance, and that is why I treasure that last rust-colored folding chair.

Tradition
is the practice of handing down stories, beliefs, and customs from one generation to another in order to establish and reinforce a strong sense of identity.

As I (Otis) spoke of the traditions established in our family, I noticed Skip, a friend of our children, had dropped his head. His chin, resting on his chest, led me to think something was wrong. I asked if I could help. He mumbled something inaudible. I stretched my hand toward the sixteen year old, put my fingers under his chin, and lifted his face to see his eyes. Before I could speak he informed me of his hopelessness. My excitement for traditions had magnified the fact that he had never experienced them in his family, or known his father.

We began to talk. Skip told me what I've heard from many other people in similar situations: "It's too late for me. I have nothing to pass on."

"Not true!" I told Skip.

We are given beautiful examples from Scripture in the lives of Joash (2 Chron. 24) and Uzziah (2 Chron. 26). These men both had fathers who abandoned Hebrew traditions and followed pagan customs. But neither, even as young kids, allowed that seemingly hopeless fact to hinder his resolve to follow the right way. Each of these men established valuable traditions for his own family *and* for the nation. The key factor is that each gained by *giving*. Joash and Uzziah returned lost traditions and found they received a legacy too.

If you find yourself wearing the same shoes as Skip, don't despair. You can repair the breach in your connection to the past. It is never too late to create a family legacy for yourself and your future loved ones by being purposeful in giving what you didn't receive. You can begin establishing traditions today.

You Want to Leave a Legacy

You have picked up this book because you are part of the growing movement who want to leave an inheritance for your children, and *their* children. You want to leave more than money—you want to leave a legacy. Our goal is to offer practical and biblical instruction, as well as inspiration, to parents who want to pass on a godly heritage. God designed families to help each member discover who he or she is in the rich tapestry of family heritage. Parents and grandparents are in a unique position to provide the environment and nurture for that.

Traditions are the family's God-ordained vehicle to pass on a positive heritage. It doesn't cost a lot of money to pass on valuable traditions. But it will cost time, thinking, and the courage to move from ideas to action. It is our prayer that this book will launch a movement of families who will establish traditions as a way of fulfilling their responsibility to impress spiritual truth on children. As you read *Family Traditions*, may you discover and develop your own special customs and events to impact your children's identity and values. You may even decide to go to Sears and purchase a folding table and chairs!

Chapter 1

A Legacy of Tradition

When my (Tim) grandmother died, everything she owned could be packed into a cardboard box. She had already given most material possessions away. But an inheritance is more than things that can be included in a will. And an inheritance is not lost even if a person receives nothing at all. Otis helped Skip believe he could begin to create one by purposefully planning for his future family. Always, an inheritance is created and communicated through traditions, many of those passed, like food, around a simple folding table.

PRINCIPLE : Traditions affirm worth, give identity, and communicate values.

INTENTIONAL IMPACT: I will take the initiative to develop family traditions for my children and grandchildren that will communicate a godly legacy, leaving them a rich heritage.

The first time Jack came to see me (Tim) for counseling, no one would have guessed he was a successful physician. His eyes were bloodshot, puffy, and underscored with dark circles.

He walked into my office saying something about "needing advice on how to deal with the kids." As he plopped down in a chair, he let out a sigh. I recognized it as a sigh of despair.

"I don't want my kids to suffer from the divorce," Jack told me. "We're in the middle of it."

"I am sorry to hear about that," I said.

"Yeah, me too. I just don't get it; my wife says she found 'someone else.'"

"Ouch—that must hurt."

"Too much for words. I can't figure out what went wrong; I was successful at school, at the hospital . . . I guess I wasn't too successful at being a husband."

"And you hope things will be different for your kids."

"Exactly!" Jack said.

"Then let me ask you a question. What will you do differently than your parents did?"

Jack's forehead wrinkled. "What do you mean? What do my parents have to do with my kids?"

"Well, interpersonal skills are influenced by the way we were raised," I told him. "People given a rich emotional legacy feel equipped to take on relationships with confidence. And they pass that on to their kids. If no legacy is created, relationships are poorer—and parents pass that on too."

"I didn't get much emotional support growing up. My mom and dad's approval depended on how well I did at school and sports. If I didn't excel, there wasn't much affection and affirma-

---

.....

Birthday Breakfast

We have a large birthday banner that I put up the night before (while the kids are in bed). Wrapped presents are on the child's place mat; the gifts are opened at breakfast. A muffin with a candle in it is on his plate!

Jeannette James, Camas, WA

.....

tion. I had to earn their approval. I'm better at competing than relating."

"Do you think it affected your marriage?"

"Yeah. My wife accuses me of not *investing* in our marriage and family. She says I was too focused on work."

"And you still want to salvage the time left with your kids?"

"Yes, before they reach the age when they don't want to be seen with me in public." A small smile surfaced on Jack's face.

"I know what you are talking about," I grinned. "I have two teenagers."

"But how can I give my kids something I didn't receive growing up?"

"You don't have to receive a rich emotional legacy to give one. Family legacy is that enduring sense of security and stability that is nurtured in an environment of safety and love regardless of performance."

"How can I make that happen for my kids?"

It took time for Jack to understand and implement the fundamentals of creating a legacy based on family traditions. We started at the beginning as he tried to understand his children's world, feelings, and concerns. He learned to listen—really listen—when they told him about their day. He began to look for things they might enjoy together, and spent time doing those things with them. Jack had to learn what it takes to model emotional honesty with his kids, letting them know emotions aren't right or wrong, just signals of what is going on. He also got involved in a divorce recovery program through a local church, where he received support and instruction for himself. Then he began to slowly build a legacy of togetherness for his kids by creating traditions around the spiritual, emotional, and social aspects of his new kind of family life.

A Rope With Three Cords _____

Every family legacy has three distinct yet interrelated parts, like a rope with three cords: spiritual, emotional, and social. These cords secure a person to the past, give ballast in the present, and help him look with hope into the future. The wise king Solomon said, "A cord of three strands is not quickly broken" (Ecc. 4:12). Together, the cords are stronger than any one or two alone. Each cord is essential and influences the other two. They are intertwined and interdependent. We will see in our children exactly what they have seen in us. Let's look at how each cord contributes to a strong family heritage.

The *spiritual* cord is the process of modeling and reinforcing the unseen realities of life. Many families neglect this vital aspect of heritage, dismissing it as "religious," "unnecessary," or "irrelevant." Yet every human being is made in the image of God with a built-in hunger for connecting with Him. Those without a spiritual cord are destined to have a weak sense of identity and purpose. Spiritual legacy is more than baptism, a camp experience, or deliverance from tragedy. It is integrating God's timeless truths into our everyday experience as a family. It is usually *caught* rather than *taught*. Our children observe in us, their parents, the truth of spiritual realities by watching how we live.

The *emotional* cord creates an atmosphere of security and love at home, preparing children for the challenges of life. We've met many adults suffering the long-term effects of a painful childhood, now crippled with a negative emotional legacy. Insecure, feeling unloved, and desperate for approval, these adults are not equipped for the roller coaster of life's ups and downs. The emotional cord provides the connection of belonging and approval. When a child feels connected to her parent(s), she sees herself as competent, capable, and supported. This emotional cord is woven over time through a parent's expressing unconditional love and acceptance to offspring. It is woven by communicating in a variety of ways, "I will always love you—no matter what."

The *social* cord means teaching a child the skills necessary for cultivating healthy, stable relationships. I've seen children who are in emotionally healthy Christian homes (the first two cords), but are handicapped by an inability to relate to other people. Those who are able to make friends and keep them have an edge in the game of life. Those who don't are limited; they have a loss of freedom and resources. Instead of feeling blessed, they almost feel cursed by isolation and loneliness. The best way to pass a social legacy to your child is to model it. Let him see you demonstrate respect, responsibility, compassion, and boundary setting. When you teach children to relate effectively and solve conflict, you are preparing them for marriage and a family of their own.

> •••••
>
> ## *Milestone Letter*
>
> For my sixteenth and eighteenth birthdays, my family and significant others wrote letters affirming the growth they had seen in my life. They noted the growth of my character and evidence of spiritual growth. They reflected on the past and anticipated a favorable future.
>
> *Robin Spurlock, Corralitos, CA*
>
> •••••

A Father's Legacy

A child who is entrusted with the treasure of a rich family legacy involving all three cords is likely to pass on the treasure to future children. Here is the story of one dad told by his son Ryan, who was sixteen when he spoke at his father's funeral.

> *My dad died on Easter Eve of a massive heart attack. He was only forty-three years old. But before he died, he prepared us. You see, my dad gave me and my brother, Sean, three things*

that will help us through life.

First, he loved us. My dad was my best friend. The night before Easter, he came and sat on my bed and talked as he did every night. He said, "Ryan, I love you, and I always will." Six hours later, he died in his sleep.

Second, Dad loved God and His Word. He took us to church, read us the Bible, taught us about God and how to pray. I know God will get us through this, because I know God the way my dad did.

Third, Dad taught us to serve others. He taught fifth- and sixth-grade Sunday School for years. He really loved those kids! We have learned to be kind and serve other people from Dad's example.

This is what I have learned from my dad: to love your family, to love God and His Word and His people, and to serve others. Today, I am left without a dad, but I have received a legacy. Someday, I hope to pass it on to my kids.

Ryan's father was able to weave together the spiritual, emotional, and social cords of the rope of family legacy into a stronghold for his children. It will remain even when times are tough, and when as a father he would have wanted it most to hold—now that he is no longer there. Ryan's father knew that creating a heritage isn't easy for anyone, but it doesn't have to be complex. Heritage can be as simple as taking a walk with your child or sitting by his bed and enjoying a conversation. The value of it is not in what you get to keep, but in what you get to give away. It is not a treasure to be hoarded, or an entitle-

. . . . .

𝒜dvent Straw

We put a piece of straw in a basket manger each time we do something kind that "welcomes" Jesus into our home. On Christmas Eve, we place Jesus in the manger.

Lori Davis, Wheaton, IL

. . . .

ment to be savored, but an inheritance to be passed on with joy. The paradox is, when you are growing and giving, you discover that you receive a heritage—even if it did not come through your own parents. The heritage is something with which God graces you because of your diligence to your children and obedience to Him.[1]

What Is a Heritage? _____

Heritage
is the spiritual, emotional, and social legacy that is passed from parent to child with its positive or negative impact.

We like to tell people, "You have a choice about what you will pass on to your kids: a *lunacy* (the craziness and dysfunction that may have been handed down to you) or a *legacy*—a rich spiritual, emotional, and social inheritance. Which will it be: lunacy or legacy? You may have inherited what appears to be a generational curse from your parents or grandparents, but according to God's Word, you don't have to be trapped there."

See, I am setting before you today a blessing and a curse—the blessing if you obey the commands of the Lord your God that I am giving you today; the curse if you disobey the commands of the Lord your God and turn from the way that I command you today by following other gods, which you have not known (Deut. 11:26-28).

You can experience God's blessing if you choose to obey His commands. God entrusts you with the powerful use of choice. You have the ability and freedom to make choices that will impact your own life and the lives of your children. You can pass on God's love and blessing. His big idea is that you *get* by *giving*. Jesus said, "Give, and it will be given to you" (Luke 6:38). As you seek to build a strong heritage for your children, you build one for yourself. As you focus on being an instrument of blessing to them, you discover that the process becomes a source of blessing to you. As you seek to understand and follow God's principles for living in your family, you receive the heritage He has in mind for you.

Which do you want? A blessing or a curse? The choice is yours.

A blessing is to hope for spiritual power, success, fruitfulness, and longevity. It grows from freedom and resources in a person's life. It is a proclamation for a rich and abundant life. It is a bonus.

A curse is divine judgment for breaking God's law. It means experiencing the natural consequences for sin and punishment for disobedience. A curse is a loss of freedom and resources.

Which would *you* choose?

We can't influence what was handed to us, but we can choose a different future for our children, if necessary. The influence of ancestors is more than the passing of physical characteristics. It impacts spiritual lives positively or negatively. God has left with you and me the choice of what to pass on. The choices we make about life today positively or negatively impact our children and their offspring. This concept is so critical that as God gave the Ten Commandments, He instructed Moses to teach the nation Israel about influencing generations:

> *I, the Lord your God, am a jealous God, punishing the children for the sin of the fathers to the third and fourth generation of those who hate me, but showing love to a thousand generations of those who love me and keep my commandments* (Deut. 5:9-10).

God makes it clear that He allows the consequences of ancestral sin to impact several generations. Certainly we see families where dysfunction has been passed down. But God desires to redeem that legacy, so blessing will replace it in the next generation, just as when our forefathers' and foremothers' love and obedience to God brings blessing. The good news is: the sin of others can be redeemed by the choices you make, *and the blessing is greater than the curse!*

The Heritage Tool Chest

Once you have decided to be intentional about passing on a heritage, you will want to make use of the Heritage Tool Chest. Flip open the latch and peek inside. You will be greeted first by a waft of pleasant aroma. This is the *family fragrance,* used to create a loving atmosphere in the home. It includes the five sweet-smelling elements of AROMA:

Affection
Respect
Order
Merriment
Affirmation

If a home has these five qualities, it will be a place of tranquillity, harmony, and enjoyment. (To learn how to create a sweet AROMA in your family, see J. Otis and Gail Ledbetter's book, *Family Fragrance.)*

The second tool we discover in the Heritage Tool Chest is a set of *impression points.* These are opportunities to make an impression upon children—impressing them with who we are, what we think, and what we do. The impressions may come through words, but they contain more power and lasting effect when

. . . . .

Grandma's Mother's Day

We used to buy my mother flowers and seeds, then the kids and I would help her plant them. For months, she would have a reminder of our love for her anytime she picked a flower.

Rose Yancik, Colorado Springs, CO

. . . .

they come through instructive events children can observe. Occurring incidentally, or intentionally created, we use them to impress upon children our values, preferences, and concerns.

One popular application of *impression points* is Family Night, a weekly time of games, conversation, study, laughter, and activities designed to reinforce the importance of family and faith. Children learn best when they are active participants, rather than passive observers. Family Night gets everyone involved. (For more ideas, see *An Introduction to Family Nights* by Jim Weidmann and Kurt Bruner.)

The third tool in our Heritage Tool Chest is the *right angle*—a tool that lets us draw a perfect vertical line to show our children what is right. It is the standard of normal, healthy living against which our children will be able to measure their attitudes, actions, and beliefs. In a pluralistic and relativistic culture, we need a plumb line that is authoritative and reliable, providing security and a trustworthy standard. The *right angle* must be based on truth that has withstood the test of time in generations and cultures, relevant for all people. That plumb line is God, and the *right angle* is His Word, the Bible.

Fourth, we find a set of *traditions*. Like a set of sockets, we need more than one. There will be different *traditions* with different applications, depending on the job at hand. A strong heritage doesn't just happen. It can only be created by having a plan, and with intentional effort. Family traditions are used to build and maintain a healthy sense of identity by passing on an understanding of who we are and where we have come from. (For further description of the tools, see *The Heritage—How to Be Intentional about the Legacy You Leave*, by J. Otis Ledbetter and Kurt Bruner.)

Chapter 2

A Longing for Tradition

◠◡◠◡

*M*y throat was parched and my hands were clammy. Even though the air conditioner was running, I was perspiring. *Was I doing the right thing? Had I made the right choice?* Perched on the Naugahyde sofa, I launched into some last-minute self-analysis. The more I pondered, the more anxious I became.

The door creaked open.

"Good afternoon, I'm Pastor Baxter."

"Yes. I'm Tim and this is Suzanne." I offered my moist hand.

"Congratulations on your engagement." A hearty smile spread across his broad face. "Thanks for coming in. We think premarital counseling is important in the commitment you're making."

"Thanks, that's why we're here too."

The pastor presented an overview of the premarital program, then asked, "Do you have any questions about the ceremony?"

"Well," said Suzanne, "yes, we do—about the music."

"Our church policy is basically no secular music after the candles are lit. We want the focus to be spiritual."

"Okay," responded Suzanne slowly, "we were . . . just

wondering . . . umm . . . if we could have a special family song. We love the movie *The Fiddler on the Roof*. It has so much about Jewish traditions," she explained.

The pastor's eyes focused on me. He seemed to be studying my dark curly hair. "I know, something about traditions helping the Russian Jews to keep their balance, like a fiddler on a roof?"

I agreed, quoting, in my best Russian accent, "'I can tell you in one word— TRADITION! Because of our TRADITIONS, we've kept our balance for many, many years. We have traditions for EVERYTHING! And because of our traditions, every one of us knows who he is, and what God expects him to do.'"

"Since it means so much to our family, we would like to have a bit of Jewish tradition in our ceremony," explained Suzanne.

The pastor's eyebrows raised. "What do you mean?"

Suzanne responded confidently, "We would like to have the song *Sunrise, Sunset* sung as the two families come down the aisle. Tim and his family will come from the front, my family and I will come from the back."

The pastor pondered for a long minute, then responded, "Since it is part of your heritage and everything," nodding at me as he studied my Jewish-looking features, "I suppose we could make an exception this once."

On our big day a few months later, Suzanne and I enjoyed some songs and other elements of a Jewish wedding. I never told Pastor Baxter I wasn't Jewish. (Some things are just as well left unsaid!)

Suzanne and I have seen several stage productions of *The Fiddler on the Roof*. One of Tevye's lines summarizes the play: "Without traditions, our lives would be as shaky as a fiddler on the roof!"

In a harsh land, in uncertain times, traditions were a source of solace for the poor Jewish milkman. As revolution threatened to change the political climate, Tevye sought to keep some things stable and secure for his wife and daughters. He was thinking he may not be able to stop the revolution in his country, but he certainly wouldn't allow it in his home! Traditions gave him a sense of time and place. They shaped his identity and helped him feel secure. He assumed his daughters would adopt his beliefs because they kept his traditions.

But Tevye was mistaken. His three daughters didn't keep his traditions. Instead of accepting an arranged husband, his oldest daughter wanted her childhood friend and admirer to ask permission to marry her. Tevye protests: "How can they choose one another? It is a father's role to arrange a husband for his daughter!" He eventually relents and grieves the loss of a time-honored tradition. At *least,* he reasons, *he is a nice Jewish boy.*

> .....
> ## A Quiet Christmas Eve
> When the children were young, we'd always go out for a nice dinner on Christmas Eve. It was good to have that quiet time, after all the stores have closed, reflecting on what Christmas is really all about.
> Martha Bolton, Simi Valley, CA
> ....

The challenge of traditions continues with Tevye's second daughter, who befriends and falls in love with a non-traditional Jew. But this time it is even more difficult for the tradition-loving father. The young man *announces* to Tevye that he is going to marry the young woman. "How can they *tell* me? The father must be *asked!*" Tevye struggles with this new way of thinking, but eventually gives in and offers the newlyweds his blessing. He doesn't want to lose a daughter over a tradition that seems archaic to the young people.

As each of these traditions erodes, Tevye loses his stability and sense of place. He isn't sure of his role in this strange, new world. Things get worse for him with the third daughter. It wasn't that she ignored an arranged marriage, or fell in love with a nontraditional Jew—she does the unthinkable, the one thing that breaks with all good Jewish tradition: she falls in love with, and marries, a Gentile. No common legacy. No shared roots. No compatible beliefs. His daughter pleads with him to acknowledge her choice. But it would mean giving up too much. Tevye needs traditions to keep his balance in a shaky world. Without them, he loses identity and purpose. Tevye walks away from his daughter in grief and confusion.

The fiddler slips off the roof. The music is silenced.

A Loss of Roots

What happened in *The Fiddler on The Roof* isn't isolated in a play about a Russian milkman. It is happening in homes across North America. In our passionate pursuit of individualism, we have lost connection to our roots. It is healthy for children to grow up, define themselves separately from their parents, and learn to make it on their own. But the pendulum may have swung too far in our western culture. Like Tevye, we have lost our sense of time and place. Like Tevye's daughters, we have abandoned the impact of a strong heritage in favor of individualism. As a culture, we esteem the individual who works hard, takes risks, and travels alone, but in our fascination with the *Lone Ranger* motif, we have lost sight of the value of community. We are pragmatists, placing a high value on "whatever works," on progress and production more than relationship and cooperation. We have not understood the importance of passing on values and a strong family heritage from generation to generation. Family traditions are a means to this, connecting us with who we are and what God expects us to do.

PRINCIPLE : Identity has its roots in tradition.

INTENTIONAL IMPACT: I will create and observe traditions that will build an identity in my child resulting in a sense of what God expects him or her to do.

We like what Wes Haystead says in his book, *The 3,000-Year-Old Guide to Parenting:*

> *Western society's emphasis on individualism and progress has left many parents without the support of a value structure on which to build. When each generation of parents rejects the child-rearing dogmas of the previous generation, the result is confusion and uncertainty.*[1]

Traditions that tie us to the past and connect us with the future offer a broad perspective. They force us to look beyond ourselves and consider those who have gone before, as well as those who will come after. When people lose their customs and traditions, they lose sight of who they are and what God expects them to do. If we aren't sure who we are, how can we relate to others? How will we know what we should be about? A weak heritage produces a fragile and superficial sense of belonging, and a confused sense of purpose.

Gail and I (Otis) asked our daughter Rebecca to share about the times she was faced with life options that could have forced her to make a wrong judgment. Her answer illustrates the point.

> *Coming home from school, I always belonged! . . . I was the "in-crowd." The important people had saved me a seat, were ready to listen to my chatter, or tousle my hair. Their love for me made adolescent snubs unimportant. What is significant today as a young married woman is not that I was head cheerleader, homecoming princess, or an honor student in my graduating class, but the warm memories of my home with my siblings and parents. They gave me the ability to love others because they loved me.* [2]

The adolescent snubs Rebecca refers to are the peer pressure applied at school to make her abdicate her "right to choose" in order to be part of the in-crowd. When she refused, she was shunned. It was our obligation to create a more engaging option in our home. That option was our *unconditional love* as opposed to the *conditional acceptance* of her peers. It is the responsibility of the parent to model a moral path so inviting and inspiring that children will take the right direction in the wake of life's difficult experiences.

Don't Forget!

As Christian parents, we have the responsibility and opportunity to reinforce a strong sense of identity from one generation to the next through incorporating the discipline of traditions into our family life. We aren't implying that all tradition is good or that one should pursue tradition for tradition's sake, because some traditions can actually undermine a strong family heritage. But one of the striking themes common in the Old Testament is the "Don't Forget" theme. God did many amazing things for His people, the Israelites. But for some reason, they kept forgetting. *What was wrong with those people?* Could it be they are like us? God understands humans. He made us. He knows that we can be excited and committed one moment, bored and lazy the next. He knows we need built-in reminders.

> • • • • •
>
> ### Valentine's Day
>
> We try to have a special breakfast (heart-shaped waffles, cherry juice, strawberries), and set the table in red. We have a centerpiece made of a white box with Valentine's ribbon on it. On that box we write things we like about each person in our family, and we share our thoughts during breakfast.
>
> *Lori Davis, Wheaton, IL*
>
> • • • • •

Remember how the Lord your God led you through the wilder-
ness for forty years, humbling you and testing you to prove
your character, and to find out whether or not you would real-
ly obey his commands. . . . Beware that in your plenty you do
not forget the Lord your God and disobey his commands,
regulations, and laws. For when you have become full and
prosperous and have built fine homes to live in, and when
your flocks and herds have become very large and your silver
and gold have multiplied along with everything else, that is
the time to be careful. Do not become proud at that time and
forget the Lord your God, who rescued you from slavery in the
land of Egypt. Do not forget that he led you. . . . Always
remember that it is the Lord your God who gives you power to
become rich, and he does it to fulfill the covenant he made
with your ancestors (Deut. 8:2, 11-15, 18 NLT).

Prosperity can lead to forgetfulness. The pursuit of material
things can deaden our hearts for God. It is easy to have our
attention on what we can own and touch. We don't let a day go
by without thinking about something for our house, our car
(modern day "flocks"), or our kids (the "herd"). We think, *spiritu-*
al issues aren't so demanding; they can wait. They don't seem urgent.
The immediate quickly consumes us, crowding out the important: "Remember the Lord." "Don't forget the Lord your God."

Family traditions are God-given means to pass on a strong
heritage. Traditions are not meant to be dry, meaningless rituals,
but fresh activities that will be significant and fun. Traditions
are an inheritance that will help our descendants remember
God's acts and character.

Traditions Build Community

PRINCIPLE : Stories, beliefs, customs, and creeds meld together to
form the foundations of family traditions.

INTENTIONAL IMPACT: I will help my children stay connected to the past while reaching for the future.

The Jewish people have long been challenged to maintain their identity within a culture. In celebrating Judaism through tradition, they seek to discover meaning for life, strength for work, and comfort in distress. By celebrating with traditions, Jews have strengthened their sense of community. In Judaism, faith and people are intricately woven together. Who they are and what they believe are inseparable. A traditional Jewish prayer asks God for *binah,* or understanding. The term is related to *bayn,* meaning between. This idea is developed in Leo Trepp's book, *The Complete Book of Jewish Observance:*

> *End-of-the-Season Party*
>
> **We want to affirm our daughters when they finish a sports season: we want them to learn the value of completion. We throw a party for their team members. We show videos of their games, talk up the highlights, and offer snacks and a cake decorated around the sports theme. We invite the coach and present him/her with a gift purchased with donations from the team members.**
>
> *Chuck Hansen, Lincoln, NE*

We have to understand that Judaism has always placed the individual "between." We stand between the poles of past and future, between our individual lives and the life of our people in Israel and the world. We are impelled by the love of our forefathers to fashion the future lives of our children. We are called upon to immerse ourselves in society, and, at the same time, to retain our identity as Jews. . . . Each Jew must look at himself or herself and ask, "Where do I stand?"[3]

This is a healthy perspective. Instead of being consumed

with the individual, there is awareness that *I am between.* I am between the past and the future. I am between my personal life and the life of my family. I am between my individual life and the life of my faith community. I am between respect for my ancestors and love for my descendants. This awareness is what we call a sense of "generational place." When we become aware that our behavior and values have an impact on generations that follow, we begin to sense a responsibility to pass on a strong heritage. To pass on a heritage to our children, we must first ask, "Where do I stand?"

What is Your Tradition Quotient? _____

We have heard about IQ (intelligence quotient) and EQ (emotional intelligence); these measures seek to quantify mental and emotional capabilities. But have you ever evaluated your TQ—Tradition Quotient?

Using the following continuum, evaluate your tradition quotient. Place an O on the line to indicate your family of origin, and an F to evaluate your current family:

1	2	3	4	5
No Tradition	Little tradition	Some tradition	Quite a lot of tradition	Rigid tradition
No memories	Few memories	Some memories	Rich memories	Ritualistic
No customs or activities together	Some shared activities	Regular customs Shared activities	Predictable, shared activities	Rote, no room for new traditions We do everything together

Looking at the TQ graph, where do you stand? Do you come from a family with little or no tradition? Maybe you come from a family with *too many traditions,* one that was too rigid, too predictable, and too confining?

Understanding where you stand will help you know how to plan and develop traditions that will build a strong heritage for your family. Consider having family members respond to the

TQ exercise; it might launch an interesting discussion on how they perceive tradition.

We live in a hurried and transient culture, but the practice of traditions gives our children stability, dependability, and shared memories. These three qualities help people feel connected in relationship and community. This is critical in a rootless society. Traditions, by their very nature, are boundaries: "This is the way we do it. We don't do it that way." Predictable traditions increase our children's sense of personal security because they define a place to stand without being too rigid.

Some children may reject traditions that seem confining. You may have had a negative experience with family traditions yourself (especially if you rated yourself a 5 on your TQ). If so, you may reject the worthwhile contribution of tradition in reaction to an impersonal, rigid ritualism from your home or church while growing up. But tradition is different than ritual.

Tradition
is the practice of handing down stories, beliefs, and customs from one generation to another in order to establish and reinforce a strong sense of identity.

Ritual
is the ceremonial observance of set forms or rites, religious or otherwise.

Tradition is concerned with passing on substance. Ritual is more concerned with form. Tradition seeks to inform. Ritual seeks to conform. Rigid ritual can easily become form without function. Rituals must support the goals of tradition, not the other way around. Traditions, in contrast, should be reshaped, reformed, and continually updated to make them culturally relevant and age appropriate. Every generation faces the challenge of adapting traditions to make them meaningful and personal.

The key to all of this is not to hang onto the *form* of the family tradition, but to capture its *essence.* Meaningful family traditions retain the important values, though their shape may change from generation to generation.

Ritual might say, "We have turkey and cornbread on Thanksgiving, and play Monopoly, because that is what we did with my grandparents when I was a child."

Tradition would say, "It's important for us to enjoy a feast and recreation as part of our Thanksgiving. What are some creative ways we could do that now that you've outgrown Monopoly?"

By involving kids in developing traditions, we avoid the temptation of slipping into a ritualistic because-we've-always-done-it-that-way mentality. A meaningful tradition will be relevant and effectively inform. This implies parents will adapt traditions to the age of their children.

The Importance of Traditions _____

As humans, we are created in God's image. God is more than spirit; He is a person. He can know and be known. God has three components to His being: mind, will, and emotion. We have these same three essential components of personhood. We can think. We can decide. We can feel. Traditions are important because they validate our mind, will, and emotions. There is a divine purpose to thinking, deciding, and feeling. These are reflections of the person of God. In a culture that largely advocates an impersonal universe and the evolution of humans through chance, it is important that we reinforce the value of life and respect for humans designed by God in His image. The basic purpose of family traditions is to reinforce and clarify this in the home.

Traditions help us know our place in relationship to others. We like what Edith Schaeffer says in *Christianity Is Jewish:*

"In the beginning God." That is to say, in the beginning a Person—an Infinite Person, but truly a person. In the beginning thinking, acting, feeling, love, communication, ideas, choice, creativity. Yes, in the beginning this God who made man in His image. Personality already existing. A personal universe created by a Person. A "people-oriented universe" created by a Person. A universe with fulfillment in it for the aspirations of artists, poets, musicians, landscape gardeners, because it has been created by an Artist, Poet, Musician, Landscape Gardener. Man made in the image of One who is a Creator . . . so that man is made to be creative. Bach, Beethoven, Tolstoy, Leonardo da Vinci . . . not accidental arrangements of molecules by chance creating, but men made in the image of God who are amazing because they are men with capabilities of both appreciating what other people create, and of creating themselves, in a variety of areas. Compassion not suddenly appearing out of nowhere, but compassion already in the One who made man in His image.[4]

Christmas Snowballs

. . . . .

On Christmas Eve we light the tree and lots of candles. We turn out the other lights, then we enjoy "snowballs"—which are balls of vanilla ice cream rolled in coconut, placed on a doily and frozen. We pull these from the freezer and put a birthday candle in each. We light the candles and sing "Happy Birthday" to Jesus.

Sandy Owsley, San Jose, CA

. . . . .

A Sense of Belonging

I (Tim) was invited to a banquet by a group I didn't know too well. As I entered the hall, I was greeted and offered a nametag. People politely introduced themselves. Most had permanent, laminated nametags—mine was paper, self-adhesive, labeled GUEST with my name printed by hand underneath. The name-tag alone made me feel like an outsider. One personable woman pointed to the long table in the front, "Oh, you are a guest," she said. "You sit up there, I believe."

I grabbed a glass of punch and found a place at the head table. In a room of over five hundred people, I was feeling satis-fied with my prestigious seat. As the band played pleasant music, the head table filled in. I noticed that each person there had a permanent nametag with impressive titles underneath their names: Vice President, Chairman of the Board, Chief Counsel, The Grand Pooh-Bah, etc. I was the only paper-sticky-guy in the bunch. I felt out of place.

It turns out, I was.

"Excuse me sir," said a young woman with a clipboard, "I believe your seat is over there." She pointed across the room, toward the back, by the pillar, next to the kitchen door. Standing behind her was a distinguished-looking couple who looked a little perturbed.

"Oh, I'm sorry. I was told to sit here. I guess I'm in the wrong place." Turning crimson, I backed out of my seat, not knowing what to do with the water glass, punch glass, and nap-kin I had used. As I passed the white-haired gentleman who was waiting to sit down, I nodded, noticing his nametag: *Chief Executive Officer.* I slithered to the back of the hall. After a few bites of rubbery chicken, I slipped through the kitchen door and out to my car.

In contrast, I thought of Thanksgiving at my Grandpa Smith's. I knew my place at the folding table. I knew I belonged. I would anticipate the feast, and didn't have to worry *Will there be a place set for me? Will there be room? Where do I belong?* That sense of belonging is what I want to recreate for my future grandchildren, starting with my children today.

A Sense of "In Between" _____

In our country, there is a lot of anxiety because people don't have a sense of belonging. Whether eight, eighteen, or forty-eight years old, many are asking, "Where do I fit?" The secularists' impersonal view of origin leads many to believe *this is it; there is nothing beyond what we see and hear.* This explains the popular pursuit of pleasure and materialism. Without faith, people reason, *I'd better grab as much as I can; after all, you only go around once!* That is living life as if you are in a beer commercial. These people struggle with belonging because they don't have the sense of "in between." Not belonging to a community of faith, they don't see their role in relationship to their Creator or represent God to their children.

People of faith have the potential for a strong sense of belonging. We rejoice in connections with family, the community of faith, and the creation of God. Take your children to the ocean; let them see the beauty and power of the Creator. Take them to a field fresh with wildflowers to breathe in the natural, God-given fragrance. Take them to an art museum; let them see the intricate talent of an impressionist artist emulating the Master. Take them to a symphony to hear a hundred instruments playing in concert, reflective of things to come when we sing and play for the King of kings. These kinds of experiences help children connect with the fact that we are made in God's image. We are people of worth.

God gave us a mind so that we might know Him. He gave us a will so that we might choose Him. He gave us emotions so that we might love Him. He made us in His image because He loved us. We aren't some mass of humanity that emerged from the primal slime. We are unique creations, designed by God with the significant purpose of glorifying Him. When we affirm our personhood with our children, when we show them we belong in this world, that we have a place in it—we are helping them know God.

→ *Chapter 3* ←

Setting
Milestones

One father, wanting his son to understand the deity of
Christ, told him the story of Christ turning the water
into wine at a wedding. "This was Christ's first miracle," the
father explained, "do you understand, Son?"

"Yes, Daddy."

"So what do we learn from this story?"

Confidently, the boy responded, "If you don't have enough
wine, get down on your knees and pray!"

Sometimes kids don't catch what we are pitching.

How can we make sure our children understand what is
important to us? The answer isn't in some new parenting
method, or a best-selling manual. It is in a book, though—the
Bible. In God's Word we discover practical and effective ideas
for passing on heritage to our children. This approach isn't complex. It won't require a Ph.D. in education or psychology, expensive software or training. It isn't exclusive; anybody can use it.
God's approach to helping kids catch spiritual truth requires
something you may have overlooked: rocks. That's right.
ROCKS! We know you are thinking: *the authors have rocks in their
heads!* Close. Why? Because God told His people to stack up

rocks to mark key milestones. Whenever God did a miracle for His people, He wanted them to remember it.

So Joshua called together the twelve men and told them, "Go into the middle of the Jordan, in front of the Ark of the Lord your God. Each of you must pick up one stone and carry it out on your shoulder—twelve stones in all, one for each of the twelve tribes. We will use these stones to build a memorial. In the future, your children will ask, 'What do these stones mean to you?' Then you can tell them, 'They remind us that the Jordan River stopped flowing when the Ark of the Lord's covenant went across.' These stones will stand as a permanent memorial among the people of Israel" (Josh. 4:4-7 NLT).

We Need Stones and Stories

PRINCIPLE : Milestones are reminders and markers of our family's journey.

INTENTIONAL IMPACT: I will build milestones in order to create teachable moments that have lasting impact.

Milestones, common in our culture, help us remember the important things. When you graduate from high school, they give you a diploma. When you pass your driving test, they issue you a license. When you get married, you receive a license (and a ring) to help you remember your vows. So what's this about rocks?

Rocks were used as reminders, milestones, and monuments in Bible times. A milestone marks distance. Monuments mark a significant event. God told Joshua to use twelve stones, one for each of the tribes of Israel. These stones would serve as a memorial, helping adults and children remember what God had done for them. God never abandoned His people. He faithfully traveled with them. He delivered them from slavery. He was with them at all times. As we travel through life, we travel with God. The rocks remind us of that.

"What do these stones mean to you, Daddy?" a child might ask.

"That God is always with us, even when things seem tough. He will never leave us."

"Is that all, Daddy?"

"No. They also remind us of the many wonderful things God has done for us. These are a monument to the amazing things God has done."

"Like what, Daddy?"

That's the point! We build memorials in order to create teachable moments. We build monuments that keep fresh in our minds the wonder and majesty of Jehovah. We build milestones that rekindle our confidence in our Lord. He who walked with us in the past will continue to walk with us in the future. Our children need physical, tangible reminders of the acts and character of God. They need monuments. They need rocks.

And so do we. We are so busy parenting. Besides our jobs, we have chores to do, bills to pay, homework to help with, laundry to catch up on, and athletic events to attend, cheering on our kids. It is conceivable that between school, the grocery store, the playing field, and ballet, our kids may never prompt a discussion on spiritual issues. We can't wait for a chance encounter that might set up dialogue on important topics. We need to set

. . . . .

A Kermit Christmas

Following Midnight Mass we enjoy the *Muppet Christmas Carol* and open the out-of-state Christmas gifts. We pray for our families and enjoy pork pie, with corn and pickles— a Canadian tradition. We have an open house and invite friends without nearby family. We serve a birthday cake for Jesus.

Irene Sutherland, Widefield, CO

. . . . .

them up. We need to be intentional.

We need memorials, not just because we are busy parents, but because we tend to forget what God has done for us. It is important to carve out time from our busy schedules to reflect about who God is and what He has done for us. That is what Sabbath is all about. How important is it?

Very.

It is so important that God honored it Himself. After creating the universe, He rested. Then when He gave the Ten Commandments to Moses, He included the Sabbath in the Top Ten. Why? Because He knows we need it. He deserves our praise focus. And our kids need a protected time, one that isn't swallowed up with school, TV, soccer practice, and karate lessons. They need a day that is dedicated to God and His family. More about this later, but for now, we need to see that teaching spiritual truth to our children requires us to be intentional. It requires us to take the initiative.

Do you remember, from the previous chapter, the reference from Deuteronomy that was a warning to not forget what God has done; to not be distracted by prosperity and comfort? When we set up monuments we help ourselves, and our children, to not forget the truths that are critical to life.

Remember how the Lord your God led you through the wilderness for forty years, humbling you and testing you to prove your character, and to find out whether or not you would really obey his commands (Deut. 8:2 NLT).

Life will involve testing and challenges. We prepare our children for those by helping them observe and celebrate monuments of God's faithfulness. We might say, "See how God has provided for us? We thought that we wouldn't make it through the wilderness, but God was faithful in our trouble. He guided us and He provided exactly what we needed." This is the kind of conversation we want to have with our kids. According to

Scripture, it is our responsibility as parents to instruct children to respect the Lord and remember what He has done.

> *My children, listen to me. Listen to your father's instruction. Pay attention and grow wise, for I am giving you good guidance. Don't turn away from my teaching* (Prov. 4:1-2 NLT).

Play "I Spy"

The biblical model for teaching children involves what is called *amamanetic* instruction. (Don't worry, there won't be a test!) Amamanetic instruction includes reflective thinking with ritual and commemorative acts. It is a pile of rocks. It is a walk that talks about God. It is morning prayer. It is a good-night kiss and a prayer. It is making sacred all that happens to us. It is connecting the routine with the holy. It is integrating God into every aspect of our lives. It is taking the time to see God at work.

Have you ever played "I Spy God"? I (Tim) first discovered this game on a retreat with our youth group. We had a powerful experience of God changing lives. As youth pastor, I asked the group, "How have you seen God at work on this retreat? Respond by saying, 'I spy God at work . . .'; then describe what you are seeing." I thought we would need ten minutes for the teens to share. After ninety minutes, I was forced to conclude in order to get the students to the bus. I learned a principle that weekend that I have applied for years since—in my ministry and in our family.

When we intentionally look for signs of God's involvement and blessing in our lives, we will always discover them.

When you take time with your children to play "I Spy God," you will find Him. You may find Him working in the obvious places, but you are more likely to discover Him in the *unlikely* regions:

- Showing up as a baby in a cattle-feeding trough.

- Speaking with wisdom and insight as a twelve year old to temple leaders.

- Calling fishermen, tax collectors, and common men to be leaders in His kingdom.

- Setting up His headquarters alfresco instead of in a corporate building.

- Playing with children, tousling their hair, and making a big deal about them.

- Struggling with the demands of His mission in a garden, not at a conference table.

- Executed by a cruel Roman device of capital punishment.

- Blasting out of the grave and visiting His friends.

Jesus had a way of *not* doing the expected. Be prepared to find Him in the most unusual places. If we can discover for ourselves, and pass on the adventure of discovering God in the ordinary and the extraordinary, we will have equipped our children with a heart for His kingdom.

. . . . .

Saint Patrick's Day

We eat green eggs or green oatmeal and drink green cream soda. For dinner, we have corned beef and cabbage. We attend the festival at the Irish American Heritage Center to give our kids a feel for their Irish heritage.

Lori Davis, Wheaton, IL

. . . . .

We Are the Connectors

Parents play a strategic role in the church because they help pass on the story of faith to their children. This is their privilege and responsibility. Many parents have missed out on the adventure because they have relegated their responsibility to the pastor,

Sunday School teacher, or youth worker.

Parents, don't miss out! Be the ones to capture the blessing of discovering, with your children, what God is up to on this earth. This is a principle, fundamental to spiritual growth: *Discover where God is working and join Him there.*

> **PRINCIPLE**: Bringing historical influences to light means establishing a sense of time and place with our family.
>
> **INTENTIONAL IMPACT**: I will design creative ways to show my children that God is active in the present as He was in the past.

It is the Christian parent's responsibility to transmit to the next generation the story of what God has done. This responsibility is dynamic, not static. It isn't enough to drop kids off at church and think we have done our part. Parenthood needs to be seen as having a past, present, and future. As we parent, we bring all kinds of history and influences to bear. Hebrew thought doesn't separate old stories from current stories. God is active now just as He was then. As parents, we need to see ourselves as "in between" the lessons of yesterday and the choices of tomorrow. We are the divinely appointed *connectors* for our children:

- Connecting spiritual truth with physical human beings (our children).

- Connecting abstract ideas with rocks.

- Connecting our experience with our faith.

- Connecting God's faithfulness in the past with hope for the future.

- Connecting the choices of today with God's blessing or judgment in the future.

Have you ever thought of yourself as a *connector?* Granted, the idea is a little different. In Western culture, we are more concerned with helping our kids become independent. A more Eastern view, the view in which the Bible was written, is that parents have a responsibility to help their children *connect*. Kids need to connect to their roots, their ancestors and family history, the present, and to their distinctiveness as people of faith. They must also connect to their future, and to the plans God has for them. They are to connect with their family and the family of faith. This is an important value in Scripture, often lost in the pursuit of the individual.

> ·····
> ## New Year's Eve Plunge
> **At midnight, we have a "Polar Bear Plunge" into our swimming pool.**
> *Claudia Davis, Carmichael, CA*
> ·····

Jesus did not teach, "Children are the church of tomorrow." He didn't say, "Children *will be* the kingdom of God." He said, "Children *are* the kingdom of God." Children are the church of *today!* They don't have to become eighteen to become full members of the kingdom. They are members now! The church is an intergenerational group. The children in the Bible are the people of God. Christian children today are the people of God. There is no division between time and generations. We are all, at once, people of God.

When we view history with this relational connection, it dramatically changes our perspective. We begin to see the Bible as *our* story, not *their* story. We become part of the story. We begin to see ourselves in a crucial role of inheriting, then passing on, a legacy. Most importantly, we become less self-involved, and more God-focused. Instead of history, we begin to see it as HIS STORY.

Edith Schaeffer offers an insightful illustration:

You see the continuity continues, in the past, present and future, and although we might like to simply sit in a stadium, or a theater, and watch as lights go up and down and curtains shut off part of the history or the prophecy, and then separate to give us clear glimpses of other parts, as on-watchers, as an audience being amused or even emotionally involved, and then put on our capes or coats and go out into the midnight air and wash away the remains of emotion with a cup of coffee bringing us back to "reality," we can't. *Why? Because* if *it is* true *then* we *are a part of it all. We are a part of this moment of history, where this moment fits in to the whole scope.*[1]

We are part of His story. We are privileged to maintain the continuity of the message—the message of grace. God, in His grace, has given us children, and given us eternal life. It is our role to connect our children with God's grace. It is our responsibility to not only prepare our children for life, but to prepare them for eternity.

We prepare our children by intentionally building spiritual milestones into their lives. There are lots of opportunities as parents to take spiritual events and make them into significant life-changing memorials—if we are willing to make them priority. Understanding three stages of child development may help as you begin planning to build monuments. We will explain these developmental phases in more detail as we offer ideas in later chapters for building traditions in your family.

IMPRINT—from birth to age seven, children experience love, affection, security, and connection.

IMPRESS—from ages four to fourteen, your child's values, beliefs, and opinions are shaped by impression points.

COACH—from ages fifteen to nineteen, you can influence teens by helping them make wise decisions and preparing them for life's unpredictable situations.

Develop a Monument Time Line _____

You could make a pile of stones in your front yard every time you want to help your kids remember what God has done, but this may not be too effective. Besides, the neighbors might complain. So, what can you do to capture and celebrate your family's spiritual highlights?

Create a time line to establish monuments at the key times when your children are most open to spiritual truth:

Time Line

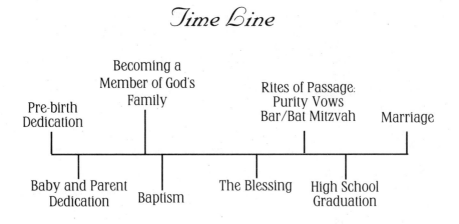

We will develop these ideas later, but this will get you started. To strategically plan monuments, consider using the following planner. The sample shows parents anticipating the exciting event of their child accepting Christ. It includes a family celebration at a later date to commemorate the event. Additional blank planners for you to use are found beginning on page 196.

Monument Planner

Event: Joining God's family

Date/age: To be determined by God

Name of child: Jessica

Purpose of event: To affirm and celebrate Jessica's salvation and her becoming a member of God's family.

Scriptural purpose: John 3:16

Theme and Scripture: New Life in Christ (butterfly theme);

2 Corinthians 5:17

Symbols and gifts:	What they represent:
An engraved leather Bible:	God's Word = new life and growth
A personal note from Dad:	written in the Bible to affirm her decision
A butterfly cake from Mom:	new life in Christ (metamorphosis)
Jewelry from Mom & Dad:	precious value of salvation

People to include in planning:	What each will do:
Grandpa:	videotape party
Grandma:	make Jessica's favorite meal
Big Brother Jim:	make a card on the computer
	for Jessica

People to invite:
Grandpa and Grandma, Amy (Jessica's best friend), Jessica's Sunday School teacher, the Schneiders (close family friends who will be godparents to Amy).

Schedule:
Sunday after church
Prayer of Blessing—Dad
Lunch—Grandma
Reading of note of affirmation—Mom
Presentation of card of affirmation—Jim
Gifts presented one at a time and explained
Circle prayer of blessing (with Jessica in the middle holding her
    new Bible)
Promise of godparents—Mr. and Mrs. Schneider
Butterfly cake—Mom
Viewing of the video—Grandpa

Budget:
$40.00—Bible, $50.00—Jewelry, $15.00—Butterfly cake, $5.00—Invitations, $5.00—Videotape, $25.00—Lunch. **$150.00—Total for event**

Capture Monumental Moments _____

Use the blank forms of the Monument Planner to develop your ideas for an upcoming event that you want to celebrate in your family. It could be for any of the spiritual monuments mentioned. If your kids are only preschoolers, don't let the idea of a wedding scare you. You have plenty of time to prepare. But start where you are. Do something to capture the significance of the current moment. Memorialize what God is doing in your family. Your kids are more apt to pick up the values to which you aspire if they see them in action—in your lives, and in a memorial that impresses them.

· · · · ·

Baby Dedication

We took *lots* of pictures. The church gave each baby a certificate and a Bible with his or her name on it. Our family went out to eat afterward.

Martha Bolton, Simi Valley, CA

· · · · ·

Dave Veerman, veteran youth worker, parent, and author, writes:

> Studies have consistently shown that children pick up the values of their parents. That is, they become most like their parents in how they live and where they invest their lives. Thus, the best way to instill in your children a love for the church is to love the church yourself. This means making worship and Christian education a high priority in your lives, supporting your local church with your involvement and money, encouraging pastors and other church leaders, and consistently praying for your church.[2]

The Main Thing _____

A good place to start building your family monuments is with a foundation of prayer. Prayer keeps us connected with God. Prayer helps us keep the main thing, *the main thing.* It focuses us on God, rather than on the logistics or implementation of the tradition. The reason we have spiritual memorials is to help our children remember what God has done for them, and who they are in Christ. The memorial is a means. The end is God Himself. A child's identity and destiny is shaped by relationship to God. We don't want the memorial to get in the way of knowing God. That is why we begin with prayer.

Ask God for wisdom as you begin to memorialize the spiritual development of your children. Ask Him to give you insight to see things as He does. Ask the Creator to help you be creative as you design memorials. Prayer as a family and your private prayer as parents can have an incredible impact on your children.

My (Tim) parents had a monument in our home. It wasn't a shrine with burning candles and small statues; it was their sacred place of prayer—their bedroom. Every night they would kneel beside their bed and offer prayers for their four children. They prayed for our salvation and maturing in Christ. They prayed for our health. They prayed we would do well at school and make wise choices with friends. I heard them pray for us not to give in to temptation with sex, drugs, and alcohol. When we started to drive, their prayers became more fervent!

I don't think my parents followed me around to check on me during my teenage years—but their prayers did. Knowing that they were praying for me created enough positive guilt to keep me from making even more foolish decisions. Their prayers guarded me from myself. Somehow, I sensed that they were turning me and my siblings over to the hands of the Heavenly Father. Then they went to bed and rested peacefully.

As a child, it is awesome knowing that you are in your Heavenly Father's hands. My parents' nightly monument before the Lord created an awareness of God's presence in my life and in our home.

My (Otis) parents, and Gail's, set markers for their children to follow. It may seem insignificant to some, but the longer Gail and I live, the more we recognize the value and deep spiritual connotations of those markers. At first, they lacked meaning for us, but we participated because we loved and trusted the people who established the markers. Among these were church attendance and financial giving. It was at church that the value of commitment was supported. As children, Gail and I were baptized, instructed, exhorted without upbraiding for our youthful mistakes, valued, and uplifted. Visiting church each week confirmed that we were connected to the functioning body of Christ. It has since become a historic monument to our own family. We have pointed to it and taught our growing children its meaning and value.

Money, or financial giving, as a monument may sound curious. Money is sometimes worshiped rather than utilized, loved rather than respected. Do we really hold to the principle that to *have* is to *give?* Do we really believe that receiving is a by-product of giving (Luke 6:38)? My parents, and Gail's, modeled this marker often so we might visit it as needed without being preoccupied by its power. We have done the same for our children, Rebecca, Matthew, and Leah.

Milestones and markers. These represent the substance of legacy for which we hope. When establishing a heritage, the visible applauds the invisible. Spiritual truth is encapsulated in practical action. An action represents a marker and a monument for all to visit, remember, copy, and point to for the next generation.

Chapter 4

Christian Holiday Traditions

*I*f you have a three year old, you've surely heard a
certain one-word question frequently: "Why?"
"Mommy, why can't the dog jump like the cat?"
"Because the cat has better springs in her legs."
"Why?"
"Because that is how God made cats."
"Can I have another graham cracker?"
"No."
"Why?"
"Because you've had enough."
"Why?"
"Come over here and pick up your toys."
"Why?"

Three is a year of *whys*. But don't panic, kids grow out of it!
At four, they don't ask "why?" any longer—instead, they simply ignore you. But that is your preparation for another stage—
that is how they will act as teens.

PRINCIPLE : To question is the privilege of children.

INTENTIONAL IMPACT: I will take advantage of my children's God-
given curiosity to introduce them to God's truth.

An Environment for "Why?" _____

The Hebrew people of the Old Testament understood this principle. They created an environment for their children to ask *why*, especially about spiritual festivals and topics.

> *During these festival days each year, you must explain to your children why you are celebrating. Say to them, "This is a celebration of what the Lord did for us when we left Egypt." This annual festival will be a visible reminder to you, like a mark branded on your hands or your forehead. Let it remind you always to keep the Lord's instructions in your minds and on your lips. After all, it was the Lord who rescued you from Egypt with great power* (Ex. 13:8-9 NLT).

As children get a little older, they will pose a more mature question. The Bible explains:

> *And in the future, your children will ask you, "What does all this mean?" Then you will tell them, "With mighty power the Lord brought us out of Egypt from our slavery"* (Ex. 13:14 NLT).

Edith Schaeffer discusses the importance of responding to our children as the Hebrews did:

> *There was meant to be not just an outward observance of some "religious rites" but as generations went on, people were meant to discuss, talk about, explain, give understanding, to their children and their children's children all that they had been told, and all that they had experienced. . . . Children are meant to be considered*

· · · · ·

Valentine's Surprise Box

A big wrapped box is in the center of the table. It has ribbons from the box to each person's plate. The ribbons are tied to a gift inside the box. Each plate has Valentines on it. After dinner, everyone pulls his or her ribbon and gets their surprise!

Sandy Owsley, San Jose, CA

· · · · ·

important, significant human beings, made in the image of God. They are meant to be communicated with, in great sections of time when parents are walking with them, sitting with them, eating with them, and continually discussing, answering questions, being interested.[1]

Consider Schaeffer's words, "Children are meant to be considered important . . . they are meant to be communicated with." To show our children they are important to God, we need to design family holiday traditions that are "kid-friendly"—ones that are fun and significant to youngsters.

. . . . .

Calendar Record

When our children accepted Christ, we had them call their grandparents long distance. We recorded the event on our family calendar and told them the angels were having a party in heaven to celebrate.

Lori Davis, Wheaton, IL

. . . . .

Use the Walk-and-Talk Principle _____

With Christian holiday traditions, we want our children to learn what the children of Israel did—that our mighty Lord is at work in our lives. That is learned by connecting the sights, smells, and activities of the holidays with deeper spiritual truths. We need to evaluate our Christian holiday traditions to see if they affirm our children and help them grow in their relationship with Christ. Our goal is to maximize the holidays to teach spiritual truth at a young age, when children are sensitive and teachable, by designing fun traditions that are age appropriate. Holiday traditions occur on an annual basis. It is then we strive to reinforce who we are as a family by telling family stories, repeating certain rituals, and highlighting the unique shared aspects of family identity. When it comes to busy holidays, the *walk-and-talk* principle is especially appropriate because it leads children to ask questions like these:

"Daddy, why is there always an angel on our Christmas tree?"

"Mommy, how come we always go caroling?"

"Why do we have such a loooong prayer at Thanksgiving dinner?"

Hear, O Israel! The Lord is our God, the Lord alone. And you must love the Lord your God with all your heart, all your soul, and all your strength. And you must commit yourselves wholeheartedly to these commands I am giving you today. Repeat them again and again to your children. Talk about them when you are at home and when you are away on a journey, when you are lying down and when you are getting up again. Tie them to your hands as a reminder, and wear them on your forehead. Write them on the door posts of your house and on your gates (Deut. 6:4-9 NLT).

Baptism

All three sons were baptized at the same time. I took pictures and cried. (Crying at major life events is a tradition!)

Martha Bolton, Simi Valley, CA

This scripture sets the tone for using holiday traditions to teach spiritual truth. The beauty of this approach is that you don't have to schedule anything extra to train your children. The *walk and talk* principle allows you to use the ordinary activities of the day. Most of the parents we talked to like the idea of integrating it into family life because it is realistic. It is do-able. It doesn't require a lot of extra time.

PRINCIPLE : Traditions are the avenue of walking and talking spiritual truths.

INTENTIONAL IMPACT: I will be alert to integrate spiritual truths into the routines of our family life, including holidays.

You may be farther along the journey of establishing healthy holiday traditions if you are already using this helpful principle. Remember:

1. Keep God the focus (the Lord is the Lord alone).

2. Be holistic: consider the emotional (heart), the mental (soul), and physical (strength) aspects of your children. Be aware of their capabilities and limitations as they grow.

3. Be intentional (commit yourselves wholeheartedly).

4. Take the initiative (talk to them, make reminders, record results in writing).

5. Incorporate traditions into your daily routine.

The passage from Deuteronomy 6 is memorized by Jewish children as soon as they can talk, and uttered with the last breath of Jews before they die. They refer to this passage as *SH'MA* or *SHEMA*. It is the affirmation of the covenant or agreement describing the connection between God and His people. Leo Trepp writes:

> *These verses* (SHEMA) *accompany Jews through life, giving form and unity to their existence. They are known by every Jew in every land, have been spoken aloud by untold generations, and have accompanied thousands of martyrs into death. They give unity to the generations.*[2]

"Give unity to the generations." That is our goal with Christian holiday traditions. They are the physical expressions of talking, tying, wearing, and writing about spiritual truths that Deuteronomy describes. They are our adaptation of the Jewish custom of reciting SHEMA. We want to pass on biblical beliefs and values to those who come after us. We want to maintain the unity of what we hold dear, parents to children, children to grandchildren.

Christmas Traditions _____

May I (Otis) let you in on a little secret? All seasons hold a special place, but in the fall, when the weather is nippy, and the leaves broad brushed with color, an exhilarating feeling begins to build inside me. I know that Christmas is only two months away. I know that memorable traditions are returning to center stage in our family, and they are my favorite performers. I look forward to being entertained again.

I love the anticipation of Christmas more than the day itself. That may not be a new thought, but if it is, I must warn you, the feeling is communicable. I caught it from my wife, but please, don't tell her. You see, I poked fun at her earlier in our marriage when I thought it was a malady. Now, both of us are carriers (and I'm not interested in any remedy). To enhance our anticipation, Gail and I formulated a tradition that lasted through the years. In order to spread happiness over the entire month, it was our practice to open the packages from friends and relatives the day they appeared on our doorstep. Each day during the season, the kids would rush home from school to see if any packages had arrived. The UPS truck was as popular in December as the ice-cream truck in July!

In addition, the children used those weeks to decide which package from Mom and Dad they would unwrap on Christmas Eve. From day to day their minds changed as new packages and bigger ones were placed under the tree. They knew they would be permitted to open just one before December 25. The kids are grown now, but haven't outgrown the anticipation for Christmas created through these traditions.

It has been our (Tim) Smith family tradition to have Calico Bean Chili the night we decorate our Christmas tree. It began fourteen years ago when all we had in the kitchen that night was kidney beans, hamburger, and bacon. Suzanne decided to improvise because neither of us wanted to go out into the wintry weather again. Her tasty recipe stuck as tradition—until this year. Brooke and I brought home a beautiful Noble fir. I trimmed the trunk and placed it in the stand, walked inside, and noticed Suzanne fixing dinner.

"Calico beans?" I assumed.

"No, I thought we'd take a break," Suzanne said. "I don't feel like beans. Besides, Brooke doesn't like them."

Then Nicole walked into the kitchen, "Nice tree, Dad."

"Thanks, Nicole."

"Calico beans, Mom?" She looked at the stove.

"No, I thought we'd try something different. I don't feel like calico beans."

"But it's . . . " stammered Nicole, "a *tradition*. We *always* have calico beans the night we decorate the tree," she said, her voice quivering.

I was surprised. Here was our tall sixteen-and-a-half-year-old junior in high school, begging for beans (they are good, but not *that* good!). Suzanne had underestimated the power of tradition. To Nicole, beans were an

·····

Gifts of Scripture

As soon as each of our children was old enough, he or she would memorize a passage of Scripture, and "give" it to the member of the family who was being honored at a birthday, Christmas, Mother's Day, Father's Day, or other celebration. The number of verses depended upon the developmental level of the child. Before the recitation, the child gave a beautifully wrapped package to the family member. Inside the package was a piece of paper telling what the special gift from God's Word would be. Then, the excited child stood up in front of the entire family, and proudly recited the Scripture. Loud applause, hugs, kisses, smiles, and praises of congratulations followed. The family member not only received a special and highly personal gift, but received family praise, and a gift that lasts forever. "Heaven and earth will pass away, but my words will never pass away" (Matt. 24:35).

Pat Holt, Bell Canyon, CA

·····

anticipated and nostalgic part of Christmas memories. (We didn't finish decorating the tree that night, but we did the next day—after a meal of calico beans!)

Here are some traditions you might try:

Nativity Scene

Purchase a simple nativity scene safe for little ones to actually pick up and play with. Tell the Christmas story the night you get it out, illustrating with the animals and figures.

Christmas Storybooks

Help your children understand the meaning of Christmas by reading a variety of storybooks as often as possible. Kids love the pop-up books. It is a Smith family tradition to buy a new Christ-based book every year, and put out at Advent. We are not opposed to just-plain-fun storybooks, either. *The Night Before Christmas* is one of our favorites. Every year, we buy a new version of it, and starting the night we decorate our tree, a different child gets to choose which version she wants to read. (If you don't want to include Santa in your Christmas, skip this one.)

A Holiday Activity Plan

Have you noticed how busy it gets at Christmas? In the late fall, ask each family member to write or draw (on a 3 x 5 card) two or three events, activities, or ideas they would like to do during the season. Collect the cards and call a family meeting. Say, "We want to plan Christmas to be an enjoyable and peaceful time. We want to do some special things, but we can't do everything. We can't go to every party. We can't go see every play. So let's decide, as a family, on a Christmas plan."

Go through each of the cards and place a cross next to the ideas that focus on Christ—after all, it is His birthday. Make sure each family member has at least one idea selected. Say, "We want to have our minds on Christ at Christmas. Here are the ideas that seem to do that best." Read the ones with the cross beside them. Include them on a master list: "Christmas at Our House" on green construction paper cut to look like a Christmas tree.

The Love Gift

Open one gift each on Christmas Eve. It could be a low- or no-cost gift like a special photo in a homemade frame, coupon for a free backrub, chore, video and popcorn date, or a promise of time/shared activity. It might be a fishing day, bike ride, walk to the ice-cream store, or three uninterrupted hours in the mall for after-Christmas sales. Be creative. The point is to communicate love in a language that is meaningful to the recipient. This might be a good time to pass along family heirlooms—those with real or sentimental value (Grandma's pin, Father's pocketknife, a cherished quilt). It could be a rite-of-passage occasion when an older sibling passes on something he has outgrown to a younger brother or sister (electric train set, video games, dolls, special dresses, toys).

Advent Calendar

Purchase a calendar that counts down the number of days to Christmas (inquire at your local Christian bookstore). Some Advent calendars have candy behind each door. Others suggest ideas for celebrating a Christ-centered Christmas. Open a window on the calendar each day after breakfast (try including cranberry, berry, or cherry juice) to get you in the Christmas spirit.

Happy Birthday, Jesus

Wrap a box, make a small slot on the top, and place in front of your Nativity set. Ask each family member to place money in the "Jesus Box." Take it to church on Christmas Eve or give to a worthy cause or a needy family, as your family's birthday gift to Jesus. One family used the money to purchase food and small gifts for another family, surprising them by caroling and presenting the basket of goodies.

Bake a cake and decorate it, "Happy Birthday, Jesus," with Christian symbols. Create a party atmosphere and invite your children's friends. Play festive music and pass out candy canes, reminding children that the "J" shape of the cane is to remind us of Jesus.

Christmas Card Prayer Box

Have your children decorate a shoebox with wrapping paper and homemade stars or Christmas symbols. Place this on your dining table. As you receive Christmas cards, place them in the box. Before meals, take out a card and pray for that family when you thank God for the food.

Christmas Media Basket

The Smith family has a red basket to hold Christmas CDs, tapes, and videos. They frequently serve hot chocolate and popcorn for an evening of music in front of the fireplace, or snuggle up on the couch for a video. *Miracle on 34th Street*, *It's a Wonderful Life,* and *Little Lord Fauntleroy* are favorites.

Advent Wreath

Advent is Latin for "a coming." It refers, of course, to Christ's coming to Bethlehem. An Advent wreath with five candles (four of the same size and one taller) helps children prepare for Christmas by thinking about what Christ offers. You can purchase or make one (check the craft stores). Each week, focus on a new theme. Use the Advent tradition here, or adapt it for your family.

WEEK ONE: HOPE

On the first Sunday of Advent, light the first candle representing HOPE. You might say to your children:

PARENT: Today is the first Sunday in Advent. Advent means a coming. What is coming up?

CHILD: Christmas!

PARENT: Christmas is Jesus' birthday party. We are so glad He came. Because He came, we have hope.

CHILD: (Lights the first candle of the wreath.) Why do we light the candle?

PARENT: This is the candle of HOPE. It reminds us of the hope we have in Jesus, and the hope we have because He is coming back to be with us. He likes to be with us. (Read Isaiah 9:6-7.)

PRAYER: Dear Heavenly Father, thank You for sending Jesus to be our Wonderful Counselor, Mighty God, and Prince of Peace. Because of Him, we have hope. We anticipate Christmas with hope because of

Jesus. We anticipate and are excited about His return. Amen.

ACTIVITY: Hope Chain—materials: construction paper, scissors, Bibles, and tape. Cut construction paper into strips (one for each day until Christmas) $1^1/2$ X 6 inches. Give each person at least three strips.

Say, "Christmas is a time of hope. We have hope because God keeps His promises. Let's see if we can find some of His promises." Look in the Bible for promises from God. When you find one, write it on the strip or draw a picture of the promise. Have older children or adults help younger children. After you complete your strips, ask everyone to share a promise they discovered. Begin building a Hope Chain by linking each strip with another strip (tape or staple the ends to secure the circle).

WEEK TWO: PEACE

PARENT: Christmas is a celebration of Jesus' coming—to Bethlehem and into our lives.

CHILD: (Lights the first candle.) Why do we light this candle?

PARENT: The first candle reminds us that Jesus Christ is our HOPE.

CHILD: (Lights the second candle.) Why do we light this candle?

PARENT: The second candle reminds us Jesus came to give us PEACE in our hearts. (Read John 14:27.)

PRAYER: Thank You, Jesus, for coming to give us peace. We don't have to be troubled or afraid. We can have Your peace in our hearts. Help us to experience Your peace this Christmas and not to be so rushed or busy that we miss You. May Your peace guard our hearts and minds as they are focused on You. Amen.

ACTIVITY: Using foam core board (white sponge-like board you can get at craft and drugstores) make cut-out sheep, representing the Good Shepherd, angels who appeared to the shepherds, and doves symbolizing God's peace throughout Scripture. Use craft hangers to make ornaments for your tree or a coat hanger and fishing line to make a PEACE mobile.

WEEK THREE: LOVE

Celebrate God's love for us.

PARENT: We are celebrating Advent—the coming of Christ. He came because He loved us.

CHILD: (Light the first two candles.) Why do we light these two candles?

PARENT: The first candle reminds us Jesus is our HOPE. The second reminds us Jesus is our PEACE.

CHILD: (Light the third candle.) Why do we light the third candle?

PARENT: The third candle represents God's great love. God showed how much He loved us by giving the very first Christmas present. He gave us His Son—Jesus.

CHILD: Why did God give us His Son?

PARENT: So that all people can be saved. So that we could know God and be close to Him. He loves us that much. (Read John 3:16—have your children recite it if they know it.)

PRAYER: Thank You, Heavenly Father, for sending Your Son to save us. We know You did that because You love us. This Christmas, help us remember Your love, and to love others as You loved us. Amen.

ACTIVITY: Bake Christmas cookies using cutters to make symbolic shapes. Decorate them, and hand deliver to neighbors or friends in small baskets or bags: "Sending you a fresh greeting to celebrate the love God sent us when He sent Jesus." Or do a variation of "Doorbell Ditch"—ring the bell and run (like a Christmas angel)!

WEEK FOUR: JOY

Celebrate the joy of Christ's coming.

PARENT: This is the last Sunday in Advent. We are excited about the coming of Christ!

CHILD: (Light three candles.) Why do we light three candles?

PARENT: The first candle reminds us Jesus is our HOPE. The second stands for the PEACE Jesus brings. The third candle represents God's amazing LOVE for us.

CHILD: (Light the fourth candle.) Why do we light the fourth candle?

PARENT: The fourth candle is the candle of JOY. It reminds us of the singing of the angels and the joy we have when we come to know Jesus. Jesus is our source of joy. (Read Luke 2:8-20.)

PRAYER: Dear Heavenly Father, we thank You for the good news of great joy, for everyone. The news that Jesus is for everyone. Because He came to earth, everyone can know You by knowing Him. With joy we declare, GLORY TO GOD and peace on earth to all whom God favors. Amen.

ACTIVITY: Play Christmas Charades. Prepare small pieces of paper with the names of characters in the Christmas story (donkey, sheep, cows, innkeeper, etc.). Place these into a bowl or hat. Each family member pulls out one, but doesn't show it to anyone else. (If a child is too young to read, whisper the name of the character.) Act it out without using words (animal noises might be allowed). See if the rest of the family can guess who it is. Optional: if someone guesses right, they get an extra cookie.

CHRISTMAS DAY: JESUS HAS COME

Celebrate that the good news of great joy for everyone is JESUS!

PARENT: Jesus has come! He is our Savior of Hope, the Shepherd of Peace, God's gift of Love, and the baby that brings the world Joy. Light all the candles!

CHILD: (Lights all candles.) Why do we light this tall candle?

PARENT: Because Jesus is King of kings and Lord of lords. He deserves the top place.

CHILD: Jesus is Lord.

PARENT: We light this candle because Jesus is the

source of all life. He came to give life. When we know Him we gain eternal life and we don't have to walk in darkness. Jesus is the light of the world. (Read John 8:12 and John 10:10.)

PRAYER: Thank You, Jesus, that You are the light of the world. We don't have to walk in darkness anymore. Thank You that You came to save us. Heavenly Father, we are glad to be Your children. We receive Your great gift of grace and love in Jesus. Amen.

TOGETHER: HAPPY BIRTHDAY, JESUS!

ACTIVITY: Enjoy the day of celebration with your family, remembering that He is the reason for the season.

Here are other holiday traditions from Christian families:

Easter Celebrations

Special Eggs

When we color eggs with the children, we leave one pure white one to represent Christ's sacrifice for us. It made us forgiven and sinless in God's sight. We also include our dog, Spot, in our backyard Easter egg hunt. He gets eggs fashioned from Gaines Burgers! *Lori Davis, Wheaton, IL*

Spring Branch

We place a flowering branch in a prominent place in our house and decorate it with eggs blown empty, painted, and decorated by our family. *Virginia Polley, West Des Moines, IA*

Thanksgiving Celebrations

"Corny" Thanks
We give each person five kernels of corn and ask them to come up with a thank You to God for each one. We record these in writing for our memory book. We remind the children that the pilgrims actually did this at the first Thanksgiving dinner. *Claudia Davis, Carmichael, CA*

Place Cards
Choose a Bible passage on thankfulness; split it up by writing one phrase on each of several place cards. Ask everyone to read their section in order as a Thanksgiving prayer. *Julie Hammonds, Colorado Springs, CO*

Kitchen Reminder
I make a chart and have everyone write down what they are thankful for at Thanksgiving dinner. I hang the chart on the refrigerator for the rest of the year. *Martha Bolton, Simi Valley, CA*

Personal Affirmation
Before enjoying our feast, we go around the table and share two things we are thankful for about the person on our left. *Sandy Owsley, San Jose, CA*

→ *Chapter 5* ←

Establishing Traditions Year Round

rooke and I (Tim) played basketball tonight after dinner, then sat down in the living room to talk. As she chatted about her basketball team, I noticed that no longer does she have the face of a child. She is looking more like a woman. It seems like only yesterday she was in preschool. I let the scene make an indelible impression in my memory, appreciating Brooke's voice, smile, blond hair pulled back, and our conversation about something she loved. Although I needed to go to my computer and work on this chapter, I didn't rush. The words, *Don't act thoughtlessly* haunted me.

I want to be a thoughtful parent—not a neglectful one. I want to think and plan. I don't want a single moment or opportunity to just slip by. I don't want my kids to say when they grow up, "Dad had other things on his mind. We didn't seem to matter to him." As I sit down to write, it occurs to me that we parents have no guarantee of tomorrow, no assurance of anything in the future. *All we have to work with is today.* We must maximize the opportunities we have today and memorialize the moments, making impressions that will last a lifetime—through traditions. But it won't come easily.

Every Moment Counts

As parents, our days are filled with anxiety, activity, and work. We feel pulled in a variety of directions at once. We may feel uncertain of what to teach our child, or how to do it. There won't be an ideal time to teach anything. There won't be an ideal child to learn. We won't be an ideal parent to discipline and guide the child. All we have is the reality of this day, this child, and who we are as parents.

A wise parent makes the most of every moment. The Apostle Paul wrote:

> *So be careful how you live, not as fools but as those who are wise. Make the most of every opportunity for doing good in these evil days.* Don't act thoughtlessly, *but try to understand what the Lord wants you to do* (Eph. 5:15-17 NLT).

Jehovah-jireh Journal

One year my husband was unemployed. We kept a Jehovah-jireh (God will provide) journal on our kitchen table. Every night at dinner we would write what God did that day to provide (and related it to manna in the wilderness). What an incredible story it tells! To this day, it is a powerful reminder to our adult children and to us.

Sandy Owsley, San Jose, CA

Making memories will take initiative that requires openness to risk and failure. To be the kind of parent who passes on a favorable impression, we must be courageous. Tim Kimmel writes:

> *As I observe the eroding foundations of the American family, I*

*am convinced that most of the devastation can be traced to a
fundamental shortage of parental courage. The cracks in the
walls of a typical family might appear to stem from a spiritual,
moral, intellectual, emotional, or physical problem, but the
majority might have been prevented if parents had been willing
to exercise courage.*[1]

What do we need? We need:

- The courage to say *no.*

- The courage to set boundaries.

- The courage to build a close relationship with
  our child.

- The courage to be intentional about building
  family traditions.

- The courage to parent differently than we may
  have been parented.

- The courage to pass along a godly heritage.

Do you have this kind of courage?

A courageous and wise parent will look at the calendar of
the new year and see twelve gifts from God. Each month is an
opportunity to shape and mold your child into a person reflect-
ing the character of Christ. You don't have to wait for Christmas
or Easter to develop meaningful family traditions. You can do it
year round. But it will take some time. It will require you to
slow down and make the most of doing good with your kids,
even though the days are evil (and from a parent's perspective,
some days *are* evil).

If we don't seize the moment, it may slip by. Parents don't
start out with the intention of injuring a child, but the competing
demands of life make it easy to take relationships for granted in
the urgency of the moment. As Wes Haystead says, modern
society promotes the idea that faster is better. Parents who live
under the pressure of increasingly tight schedules find it diffi-

cult to slow down and spend time with a child.[2]

PRINCIPLE : Time means limited opportunities to impact my child.

INTENTIONAL IMPACT: I will do something every day, even if it is small, to create a tradition in order to pass a legacy to my child.

Many parents find it particularly difficult to spend time with their teens and enhance their relationship. At Mount Hermon Christian Conference Center, surrounded by towering redwoods, a camp provides a high-ropes course, zip line, mountain biking, swimming, boating, surfing, scuba diving, crafts, recreation, singing, pool, Ping-Pong, delicious meals, and fun chapel time for parents and teens together. But the most profound opportunities are the simple, quiet times shared between parent and teen. Any parent can do these simple things almost anywhere. Here are comments overheard:

. . . . .

Baby Dedication

For our daughter, Anne, we asked a pastor/friend back home to host a dedication service. We wrote a dedicatory prayer and performed a song for her. We selected godparents—they happened to be three godmothers—and had a big party at the church. We served food, videotaped the event (for relatives who couldn't come), and presented Anne with a certificate of dedication. She wore a custom heirloom-quality christening outfit made of French lace.

Lori Davis, Wheaton, IL

"My dad and I walked through the giant redwoods and talked for hours."

"My mom and I sat at the base of one huge tree. We didn't say much, just stared up in awe. It made us feel closer to God."

"My son lives with his mom, so I don't see him much. This weekend we were able to spend three hours together, just the two of us. I have never done that in his entire life—and he is seventeen. We sat in a boat in the creek and talked. I will never forget it."

"I will never forget the terror on my mom's face when she jumped off the platform and went screaming by me on the zip line. We laughed for hours."

A few hours together. Lives permanently changed. And we are talking about TEENAGERS here! We don't need expensive or fancy accommodations, vacations, or resources to have an enjoyable shared experience with kids.

Time as a Cycle of Seasons

We westerners have a Greek sense of time. In the New Testament, one of the Greek words for time is *chronos*. *Chronos* designates a defined period or space of time. It focuses on *length* of time, our most precious resource. It is concerned with *quantity*. As the pace of life increases, time becomes more valuable. Another word that shapes our thinking about time is the Greek word *kairos*, communicating the significance of a brief or extended moment. *Kairos* is more concerned with the *quality* of the time than the quantity. But neither of these words captures the Hebrew concept of time.

. . . . .

Training Wheels Funeral

When our sons graduated from needing training wheels on their bikes, we had a funeral for the wheels. We placed them in a cardboard box lined with black paper to simulate a casket. We celebrated by placing the wheel in the middle of the table as a centerpiece. The dinner is the child's choice (hot dogs work fine). After dinner, before it gets dark, we go outside and have an inaugural ride (without the wheels) as everyone cheers.

Dan Morgan, Newbury Park, CA

. . . . .

In the Old Testament, written in Hebrew, the word *'et* conceives of time as a series of recurring seasons or as a moment that is particularly appropriate or opportune. This eastern view sees time as a rhythm. Time has recurring cycles of days and weeks, of months and seasons and years. Life itself follows the pattern of seasons. [3]

There is a time for everything, a season for every activity under heaven. . . .

A time to kill and a time to heal. A time to tear down and a time to rebuild. . . .

A time to embrace and a time to turn away.

A time to search and a time to lose. A time to keep and a time to throw away.

A time to tear and a time to mend. A time to be quiet and a time to speak up.

A time to love and a time to hate. . . .

God has made everything beautiful for its own time (Ecc. 3:1, 3, 5b-8a, 11a NLT).

To understand traditions biblically, we must look at them with the perspective of Hebrew language and culture. Time in the Jewish outlook is a cycle—rhythmic and repetitive: there is a time for everything. If traditions are *the practice of handing down stories, beliefs, and customs from one generation to another in order to establish and reinforce a strong sense of identity,* at the foundation is an understanding of the Hebrew definition of time.

Each family goes through seasons. A wise parent, in planning traditions, considers the family seasons. Certain traditions are effective in certain seasons, and not in others. Just as the wise writer said, "There is a time to embrace and a time turn away," sometimes a hug speaks more clearly than a lecture. Sometimes time apart is more helpful than time together. *God has made everything beautiful for its own time.* The key is to discover what God wants to do in this season of your family's life.

Don't expect that what worked and was meaningful when the children were in preschool will have the same positive impact when they are teenagers. Also, don't expect that *nothing* from their younger years will have significance when they are teenagers. As wise parents, we are adapting our family customs and traditions to meet the needs of our children. We don't have to throw away the traditions. We may need simply to adapt them. As they go through different developmental stages, our children need us to adapt traditions to be age appropriate. Instead of reading a picture book at bedtime, as you did when they were three, when they are older, you can tell them a story from your life when you were eight years old. Always, make certain that the traditions are enjoyable for the changing ages of your kids.

Create a Festive Atmosphere

PRINCIPLE : There is room for merriment in all of life's cycles.

INTENTIONAL IMPACT: To show that family fun will increase the overall health of a family unit.

Who says families have to be dull? Are we more effective when we are more serious? The opposite may be truer! Families who laugh stay together. Families who enjoy being together tend to have stronger and healthier relationships. The happiest families we know are those who enjoy a common activity together and share a good sense of humor. They have discovered creative ways to include fun and festivities in their family. Not everything needs to be "spiritual." Not every moment is a "teachable moment." Some things are just for fun, valuable just for fun's sake. Some moments are just for memories—not for instruction.

Because merriment is so important to me (Otis), I set out to have a blast with our children from the beginning of their lives. When they were little, I tried to pull the wool over their eyes just to create giggles in our home. Playing hide-and-seek with Matthew when he was about twenty months old brought a lot of that. I would hide in the entryway closet every time— and he knew it. So he would come to the closet door, knock, and ask in his inquisitive little voice, "Daddy, you in there?"

"No," I would answer, "I'm in the bedroom."

"Oh," he would say, and take off for the bedroom. In a minute or two he would return and say, "No, you not."

The game would go on like that with Matthew going from room to room until he finally caught on.

> ·····
>
> ## Christmas Eve Surprise
>
> We exchange handmade ornaments, then we always read *Barrington Bunny* by Marilyn Bell. We then go out in the true meaning of Christmas, do kind acts or give gifts without telling anyone who it came from. We leave a note, wishing a Merry Christmas.
>
> *Rose Yancik, Colorado Springs, CO*
>
> ·····

Figure out ways to play with your kids—log fun time—just for the joy of it. You may be helping them prepare for life more by playing than by lecturing. Do you remember any lectures your parents gave you as a kid? I didn't think so. Do you remember times they played with you? Chances are, you do remember the fun times. They don't have to be extravagant or expensive. They just need to be what *kids* consider fun. Think carefully about how you can make each day count. Don't wait for Christmas. With a little thought, courage, and creativity, you can celebrate 365 days a year!

We can also *learn* from each other, of course, by playing

games. We learn to follow rules, compete, concentrate, work as a team, to strategize, handle defeat—and how to win without being showy. Playing games with family members isn't wasting time. It is preparing kids for life.

I (Tim) like to play basketball with Brooke. We play "horse" or one-on-one. Although now she plays on a team and is improving her skills, I used to be able to beat her with regularity. Sometimes she puts the moves on me, scoring several baskets in a row, clinching the game. It's tough on my macho, former-athlete image, but good for me to lose (I just wish it weren't out in front of all the neighbors).

Brooke's last team competition was difficult for me. They played a taller and more experienced team. Brooke's team was losing by twenty points—nothing seemed to be working. As the game continued, my frustration elevated. *Why does the other coach run up the score? Why does he leave his starters in when the other team is ahead by such a margin? Why doesn't our coach play a different lineup?* Brooke's team lost by thirty-six points. It was embarrassing and humiliating. As I slithered out, I found Brooke in front of the gym, sitting with her teammates smiling, chatting, drinking sodas, and eating from a basket of huge, fresh strawberries.

Brooke's face was stained with juice. "Look Dad, Coach gave us each a WHOLE basket!" she said. She and her teammates talked about school, boys, the weekend, movies, and the start of track season. I was still licking the wounds of my parental ego, and she was happy with a basket of berries! They didn't even mention they had just been killed on the basketball court.

Sports can help us learn to deal with life, and with defeat— even defeats that feel unfair. Sports can help us balance our perspective and learn self-control. Sports are good for families— especially for dads who have a tough time losing, even if they aren't playing. I hope that by the end of Brooke's season, I will learn what she has learned.

By now you have probably noticed that we mix the "secular" with the "sacred," and "fun" with "religious." Kids won't know the difference. That is intentional. We *don't want* our kids putting God in a Sunday/church box. As Dean and Grace Merrill say, we want them bumping into God every time they turn around, in the midst of ordinary living. That way God will stay a normal, here-and-now part of their lives in adulthood.[4] The following ideas can be used year-round. The desire to celebrate with your child is up to you!

Birthdays

Teach the significance of milestones by celebrating birthdays with pizzazz. They are unique times to affirm a child's worth and purpose. When we take the time and effort to plan birthday traditions, kids understand other important milestones in their lives.

For younger children, the most significant milestone is a birthday. They often "trade" in the economy of birthdays. They'll say, "At my party we are going to have a clown—REAL clown, not just somebody's daddy!" Or, "At *my* party I'm gonna have white cake and chocolate cake—two kinds!"

Since kids often evaluate their personal worth and status by the events of a birthday party, use this built-in assessment to affirm your child. Design elements that reinforce positive personal qualities of the birthday child. When you take time to accent your child's positive qualities, it will create a memorable experience for them. Celebrate the differences between your children. Don't be trapped by rigid traditions that say *all seven-year-old birthdays must look like this*. Study your child to discover what theme would be appealing to her. What are her favorite colors? Does she have a favorite cartoon character? What is her favorite kind of cake or ice cream? Or would she prefer nontraditional food? Some kids prefer pancakes or shish kababs!

Birthdays are opportunities to help children discover their purpose in life. We can use birthdays to shape their self-discovery and discover their mission in life. Some of you are thinking, *mission, purpose, birthdays? Those don't go together!* Typically, in our culture, they don't. But consider how influential a birthday can be. For some children, it is the only time when people, particularly their parents, are focused on them. What is said, done, and celebrated can have a huge impression. We help a child discover God's purpose when we design elements into the celebration that point to Him and how He made the child with a specific and personal purpose in mind.

You might say, "Here is your zebra cake, Jacob, just like you wanted! Black and white. Chocolate and white. Zebras look like God made them just for fun. I know you like animals, that is why I made you this special cake. Happy birthday, Jacob!" Who knows? Jacob may grow up to be a veterinarian, or a missionary to Africa!

The key is discovering your child's unique character and affirming his personhood. God made each child in a particular way. Use birthdays as a means of affirming these truths. Include your child in planning his big day. Use the following planner to ask your child's input to plan a birthday that will be meaningful and fun. For younger children, you will suggest more; older children will have ideas of their own.

Birthday Planner

Name of child: Birthdate:

Day of party:

Themes:

Favorite color:

What I want:

What I don't want:

Number of guests:

Budget:

Food:

Dessert:

Recreation:

Favors:

Transportation:

Invitations/postage:

Gift:

Siblings invited:

Adults/relatives invited:

Schedule:

Video or camera:

Monument (how will this birthday be different?):

Personal quality to affirm:

Memorial Gift (rite of passage or family heirloom):

Personal Scripture:

Birthday Journal

Purchase a blank book for each child. Record your feelings
and events about them as far back as you can remember. If
you are expecting a child, begin the journal now: write your
hopes, worries, and how you are preparing for your child.
The journal can also be used as a scrapbook. Include invitations, guest list, theme ideas, and events from each party.
Make sure you include the memorial aspects of the party,
the Scripture and any special gifts given, like this:

> *For Marsha's seventh birthday she received one of Grandma's
> quilts, and a Scripture verse cross-stitched by Mom, beautifully
> framed by Grandpa:* The Lord hears his people when they
> call to him for help. He rescues them from all their trou-
> bles. Psalm 34:17 *The theme of the party was Confidence—we
> can be comforted and confident because we belong to God and
> He is always with us!*

When your child turns eighteen, you can present the
Birthday Journal as a rite of passage: "Here is a memorial of
your childhood. We have recorded here how we celebrated
your uniqueness. You are a person of great worth, as you
can see. We have celebrated you each year. You mean very
much to us. Now, as we hand this to you, we pray that God
will continue to help you discover your purpose in life as
you walk close to Him."

Birthday Years and Guests

A simple formula for the number of guests a child may
invite to a party is to count on one guest for each year of age.
If the child is three years old, she may invite three friends.
At eight, she may invite eight friends. This helps reduce the
headache, hassle, and cost of the party. It also helps her
anticipate more growth and friends next year. We know of

many parents who try to have too many guests, resulting in the guests not feeling special. Sometimes the temptation is to invite lots of friends to get lots of presents. We teach our children an important lesson when we communicate, "This year you may have *five* special friends for your five-year-old party." Help them learn to anticipate and wait. By giving them too much, we are actually withholding life's valuable lessons.

Of course, the most challenging years come when a child is ten, and he wants TEN fifth graders tearing around the house, hyped-up from all the sugar. But that is more realistic than ten three year olds; just have the party outside—even if it's February in Minnesota!

Monthly Family Themes

Each month offers an opportunity to build family traditions around a seasonally appropriate theme, reinforced by activities, customs, and media that particular month. You might emphasize a particular character quality you want to see developed in the lives of your family members. Design a fun activity that will teach that quality.

January—Warmth

Everyone puts on their new pajamas (the ones they got at Christmas) and gathers in front of the fireplace where they are warmed by a crackling fire. Cocoa is served and the older children roast marshmallows for s'mores (graham cracker sandwiches with a toasted marshmallow and chocolate bar in the middle). Play Cocoa Circle: go around and *warm* the heart. Everyone says one nice, affirming comment about the first person. Then go on to the next. Close in prayer, thanking God for His comfort and provision.

February—Friendship

Rent a helium tank and fill colorful balloons. Make friendship balloon bouquets and attach a note of appreciation. Surprise friends (adults and children) by delivering the bouquets to them. Make Valentine cards together as a family, then deliver to friends. A fitting Scripture to discuss is John 15:13-15. Ask, "What is the greatest kind of love?" (Sacrificial.) "What are some examples of putting others first?" (Get personal.) "What does Jesus call those who love and serve Him?" (Friends.) "What do friends like to do?" (Spend time together, talk.) "What can we do to be good friends with Jesus?" (Spend time with Him, talk/pray, and listen to Him by reading the Bible.)

March—God Is in Control

Help your children understand how God's control and providence is different than luck. Make or purchase a large shamrock and tell the story of Saint Patrick, born in Scotland in A.D. 385. Patrick used the shamrock as a tool to explain the cross of Christ and the Trinity. At fourteen he was kidnapped by raiders and taken to Ireland to be a slave shepherd. Evil people (Druids and pagans) who didn't know God surrounded him. As Patrick watched sheep, he prayed day and night that his love for God would grow. When he was twenty years old, he had a dream about escaping by going to the coast. When he awoke, he did just that and discovered some sailors who took him back to Britain to be with his family.

Later, Patrick had another dream about the people of

Ireland calling him back to tell them about God. Patrick left the comfort and security of his home for the wild and evil backlands of Ireland. There he told people about Christ. Thousands—all kinds of people: kings, princes, paupers, and poor folks—became members of God's family. Patrick was courageous because he knew *God was in control.* He was more afraid of people dying without Christ than he was of the risks and rejection he faced. That is why he went back to the very people who had kidnapped him.

Ask each family member to draw a picture of his or her favorite part of Patrick's story. Share your pictures. Serve green Kool-Aid, lime Jell-O, and celery sticks with green-colored ranch dressing. Discuss Romans 8:28.

April—New Life

Visit a pet store and look at the baby animals. If appropriate, this may be the time to get a new pet and talk about it: "We need to care for, protect, and love new life." Or plan a thirty-minute drive to hunt for new life. Before you leave, ask, "Where can we go to hunt for new life?" Get a suggestion from everyone, then plan your route. As you discover new life, record it on paper, on video, with a still camera, or audiocassette. You could even make a large map and later post the photos of the new life you discovered: newborn farm animals, newly sprouted grass, buds on a tree, kittens at the neighbors', guppies in a pond or creek, baby birds at the beach, human babies at the hospital (sometimes there are viewing rooms for children). After the journey, or at an outdoor destination, break out treats (chocolate eggs, candy inside plastic eggs, bunnies, and other goodies that symbolize new life). Discuss 2 Corinthians 5:17. Ask, "What's new?"

May—New Growth

At the beginning of the month, plant alyssum; it will grow quickly. Mark your children's height on a doorpost with pencil, recording each one's name, height, and date. Go back from time to time to see how quickly they grow. Read Ephesians 4:13 and discuss what a fully-grown Christian looks like. Make a life-size poster of yourself by asking a child to outline your body on butcher paper. Color in and add character qualities with arrows pointing to different parts of the "fully grown-up Christian."

June—Celebrate Achievement

Affirm your child's accomplishments at preschool, school, or at home (potty training). Have an awards banquet. Serve kid-friendly food (hot dogs, or macaroni and cheese). Pass out homemade certificates of merit to each family member to note achievement in at least one area. Play *Pomp and Circumstance* or other graduation-type music and have a Parade of Possibility. If you have sewing skills, you could make simple gowns for your children to wear. Talk about the future and hope we have because God helps us achieve. Study Jeremiah 29:11-12 for ideas. Say, "The most important subject you could study and seek is God. When you seek Him, you will find Him."

July—Independence through Confidence

Help your child become more confident and less dependent

on you for certain things. Plan a picnic and assign each family member a responsibility: pack the picnic basket, plan the recreation, lead a hike, or be in charge of the dog. Play games that reinforce confidence and independence: hide and seek, or sardines (one person is it and hides; the others find him and hide with him until the last person finds them). At the beginning of the month, make a countdown to independence for the month. For each child, list steps of age-appropriate progress toward independence: "Tommy will tie his shoes every morning." "David will make his bed before watching TV." "Shelly will feed the dog before breakfast." "Christine will ride her bike to her friend Christa's." Make rewards appropriate for each goal. Give David a special snack to eat while watching TV if he made his bed. Let Christine go to Christa's another time if she handled riding her bike with safety.

The goal is to teach your children that confidence and independence are rewards in themselves. At the end of the month, celebrate with a Family Independence Party that affirms the growth of each member. Dad might even celebrate his independence from watching too much baseball! Buy Fourth of July decorations at half-off sales and have fun. If you decorate the front of your house, who cares what the neighbors think! Talk about John 8:36 and discuss what spiritual freedom means.

August—Connection

Family vacations and short day trips can be used to emphasize bonding and memory building. If possible, visit extended family and talk about why it's important to stay connected. If you have Lego building blocks, build a family project. Point out that Lego construction is strong because Lego blocks connect with each other. Families are sources of connection. Say, "To be strong as a family, we need to be connected." Then try building a house out of dominoes standing on their sides. They will easily fall because they aren't connected! Now build one with Legos. Talk about Ephesians 4:15-16 and how connection equals strength.

September—Discovery

Focus on the joy of learning. Prepare to return to school. Visit a museum and see what people have discovered, invented, or created (art, cars, music). Reinforce the fact that learning isn't just for when we are at school; wise people are life-long learners. A fool is a person who thinks he knows it all and loses the joy of discovery. Discuss Proverbs 13:1: "A wise child accepts a parent's discipline; a young mocker refuses to listen" (NLT). See also Proverbs 10:17. Another option might be to watch the Discovery Channel for a special TV show on the joy of learning.

October—Courage

Instead of the fear and scare tactics of Halloween, emphasize personal courage. Rent an extreme-sports video where people need courage (rock climbing, ramp skateboarding, in-line freestyle skating, snowboarding, hang gliding, skydiving, wake boarding). Pause the tape and ask, "Does what he is doing require courage?" "What is courage?" "How do you know if you have courage?" "What happens to people when they don't have courage?" An option would be to watch a video like *Chariots of Fire*. For the adventurous, try a family outing that involves a little risk, like mountain biking or in-line skating.

November—Gratitude

Teach your children gratitude to God and others by making a Thanks Gift that illustrates how someone has encouraged your child. Make an outline of the child's hands by using construction paper or plaster of paris. Then make the hands look as if they are applauding. Add a photo of the child and a symbol like a basketball, Bible, or anything that indicates the connection between your child and the person being thanked. Write his name at the top and a heading like, "My thanks to Coach Jim from Sally."

To express gratitude to God, make a Family Collage with clippings from magazine ads for all the things your family is grateful for: health, pet, car, Bible, food, family, furniture, fun together. Place the collage in a prominent spot for your Thanksgiving meal. Have one or two of the children explain the collage and why you are grateful for these things.

Create a Family Time Line of Big Events. Make a time line on poster board beginning with your wedding. Record significant events that you are grateful for: "Our first vacation as a married couple." "When we first found out we were expecting." Ask children to suggest things they are thankful for and then list them on the time line. When you have completed it, post in a prominent place. Prior to the Thanksgiving meal, read portions of Psalm 136. Note that there is a responsive reading in the chapter; adapt this to your Family Time Line. Have each family member read (those who can read) a big event in sequential order. The reader might say, "Give thanks to the Lord, for He is good!" Then respond as a family, "His faithful love endures forever." Repeat the process.

December—Giving

Counteract all the media hype on *getting* material things by designing a month focused on giving. Design an age-appropriate family service project that involves helping the less fortunate: Soup Night means instead of a more expensive meal, you serve soup at least once a week for the month, then use the money you save for a Christmas basket. Place the basket in a visible place as you fill it with canned foods, candy canes, home-baked goods and other festive items. As Christmas approaches, deliver it to a needy family. Family garage sale proceeds might go to your church or a charity. Good used clothing gathered in a neighborhood clothing collection might be donated to the Salvation Army.

Parents' Anniversary

Use your wedding anniversary to teach your children aspects of love. Sometime during the week prior to your anniversary, have a "We Are Still in Love" party. Bring out the wedding photo album, videos (if you have them), and other wedding memorabilia (invitations, veil, brochures or souvenirs from your honeymoon). Have a candlelight dinner and serve a menu that captures your early days together. Tell the story of how you met and the qualities that first attracted you to each other. After a year or two, you may want to change the format and ask the children to remember what you have told them in the past. Ask, "What first attracted Daddy to Mommy?" "Where was their first date?" "What was one of their first embarrassing moments together?"

Serve a small wedding cake for dessert and verbally

reaffirm your love for each other. Children gain security when they see their parents still love each other. This may be a good time to present an anniversary present to each other—you know, the not-too-mushy type that won't embarrass the kids!

→ Chapter 6 ←

Jewish Feasts and Festivals

⌒◯◯⌒

*T*he Jews are God's chosen people! We have heard this
statement many times, but what does it mean? Can you
imagine someone saying, "If that's what it means to be *chosen*—
with all the persecution, suffering, and prejudice, forget it!
Choose somebody else!" But God chose the Jews not for a life of
privilege and pampering, nor to be singled out for prejudice
and persecution. Our Sovereign God chose the Hebrew people
to show who He is and to demonstrate His love. Graciously
exhibiting His faithfulness, He chose to illustrate His magnifi-
cent plan of redemption upon the canvas of this small band of
folk.

> *The Lord did not set his love upon you, nor choose you,*
> *because you were more in number than any of the peoples, for*
> *you were the fewest of all peoples; but because the Lord loved*
> *you, and kept the oath which He had sworn to your fathers*
> (Deut. 7:7-8).

God chose Israel to be a *blessing* to all people. Through
Abraham's descendants, the whole world would be blessed.

Now the Lord said to Abram, "Go forth from your country, and from your relatives and from your father's house, to the land which I will show you; and I will make you a great nation, and I will bless you, and make your name great: And so you shall be a blessing: And I will bless those who bless you, and the one who curses you I will curse, and in you all the families of the earth shall be blessed (Gen. 12:1-3).

God chose Israel to declare *praise* to Him. God alone deserves our worship. We were created as praise-givers; it is part of our inherent design. Israel was chosen by God to point others to Him. We are fulfilling His purpose when we tell others about Him in order to bring *salvation* to all peoples. "The people whom I formed for Myself, will declare my praise" (Isa. 43:21).

As Christians, it's easy to forget our Jewish roots. We focus on the cross at Easter and forget that both Passover

Unique Christmas Tree Decorations

We decorate our tree the day after Thanksgiving, but we use unique ornaments that represent our special occasions and interests: chili peppers, small balls to represent our sports, tiny piano, etc.

Pam Steinberg, Monument, CO

and Pentecost were Jewish feasts before they became mighty demonstrations of God's power. To regain appreciation for our God-given Jewish roots, we want to affirm the Jewishness of our heritage. By studying the Hebrew foundation of Christianity, we will grow to value our faith with greater depth and passion.

The story of Israel is the story of God's relationship with His creation. God is a relating God. He created us in His image because He wants to know us and be known. He chose a people to demonstrate that *He* wants to be chosen by our free will. Through Israel came the holy writings. He is a communicating God who desires to connect at a deeper level with us, if we allow it. He is a God of His word. Through the drama of Israel, we learn that God makes and keeps covenants. God, in His mercy, used even Israel's disobedience and distraction as lessons to instruct generations to come about His covenant mercy. We experience God's blessing when we trust and obey Him.

Trust and obey?

Simple, and profound; but we haven't got it down yet.

That is why the Old Testament is full of object lessons. We have not fully understood, let alone trusted, all that God has for us. We, like the tribe of Israel, need regular points of accountability to keep us from drifting. God knows we have short memories, so He built in reminders to draw us back to Himself. Messianic Jews, Ceil and Moishe Rosen write:

> *Through the history of His people, Israel, we see the hand of the Almighty guiding, directing, showing what He expects of His people. Israel's customs and traditions are more than just quaint folkways to be studied by historians and anthropologists. Her history is a memorial of the past and a guidepost to the future.[1]*
>
> *Events and teachings in Scripture often have more than one meaning. There is the obvious contemporary event to which there can be one or more prophetic counterparts, and there can also be a spiritual application. The ancient feasts of*

- - - - -

Readers' Theater

Using the "Twelve Days of Christmas," we develop a short dramatic presentation that includes simple costumes and props. The real meaning of the "Twelve Days of Christmas" was used as a memory aid for learning about Christian doctrine for persecuted Christians in England in the sixteenth century. For example: Jesus was the partridge (the bird is willing to lay down her life for her chicks) in the pear tree (the cross).

Lori Davis, Wheaton, IL

- - - - -

Jehovah, which He gave to Israel, cast the shadow of a greater future reality. There was a threefold aspect to these annual festivals: first, the seasonal celebration based on the agrarian culture of that time; second, the historical remembrance of God's dealings with the nation; and third, a future fulfillment.[2]

Understanding the historical background for Jewish feasts and festivals will help us present a spiritual application for today. Developing meaningful and enjoyable traditions for our families using these, we communicate to our children who God is, what He did in the past, and what He plans to do in the future. We help our children learn a natural heart-response to God and His work because we teach them to see Him at work. We help our children sense the rhythm of God at work. We train them to walk in cadence with Him.

PRINCIPLE: Seasonal feasts communicate faith to our children.

INTENTIONAL IMPACT: I will use traditional Jewish feasts to help my children sense God at work, and learn to trust and obey Him.

In a culture that is often rushed and seldom reflective, celebrating a feast or festival provides a unique opportunity to stop our normal hectic pace, and pause to contemplate. We need to build into family life time for our children to ask:

"Daddy, why do we light the candles?"

"How come Mommy is baking the special bread?"

"What does this pile of rocks mean?"

"Why is Sunday different for our family? Jimmy's family doesn't go to church."

Children are at home for such a short time. Make these impressionable years count. As you consider planning family festivities, remember these age-appropriate goals introduced in chapter three:

IMPRINT—(ages one to seven) As we shape and direct godly values, our concerns often have to do with behavior: picking up toys, not hitting siblings, being obedient, doing chores.

IMPRESS—(ages seven to fourteen) Seeking to make an impact on the heart, we want our children's will to reflect wise choices. We want to see indications of compassion, gratefulness, and love for others.

COACH—(the teenage years) Guiding and counseling, we give up the notion that we can control our teens. We can't know what they are doing all the time. A coach offers advice, correction, and pointers, but he doesn't play the game. He seeks to influence the players.

The Key to Learning— Rhythm and Repetition

PRINCIPLE : Repetition is an effective teacher.

INTENTIONAL IMPACT: I will seek ways to repeatedly model my love for the Lord.

The Hebrews understood the value of rhythm and repetition in teaching their children. Traditions were rhythmically built into the year and the culture. There was a time and purpose for everything. Repetition reminds us of our link to God. Jewish people take seriously the words, "impress my commandments on your children" (Deut. 6:4-9). This is not an option. It is not something done with leftover energy and time. It is the focus of Jewish family life, giving continuity to their existence. The home is the training ground for Judaism. The responsibility for the spiritual development of children lies almost exclusively with the parent. A common saying from the rabbis is "there are no vacations from Jewishness." The Jewish faith is built into the rhythm of life. An expert on Jewish observances explains the importance of Shema (discussed in chapter four):

The covenant makes us one people linked to the One God. We exist because God exists; we are one because God is one. Our being and our survival rest on the love of God, and this love commits us to love Him in return. This awareness and commitment are expressed in the great affirmation of faith—
Shema.[3]

For the sake of repetition, here again is the biblical text of Shema:

Hear, O Israel: The Lord our God, the Lord is one. Love the Lord your God with all your heart and with all your soul and with all your strength. These commandments that I give you today are to be upon your hearts. Impress them on your children. Talk about them when you sit at home and when you walk along the road, when you lie down and when you get up. Tie them as symbols on your hands and bind them on your foreheads. Write them on the doorframes of your houses and on your gates (Deut. 6:4-9).

. . . . .

Jigsaw Puzzle

Between Christmas and New Year's, our family puts a jigsaw puzzle together, and glues it together for a memory.

June Berntsen, Colorado Springs, CO

. . . . .

Berakah: The Spoken Blessing _____

A Jew, as a partner in God's covenant, is called upon to make life authentic. He can't simply walk through life, but must connect the natural events of the day with the wonder and awe of the Most Holy. He must walk in harmony with God's Word, in tune with God's Spirit, and communicating with Him in continual dialogue.[4] This is why there is a blessing for every occasion. Berakah is a fixed formula of blessing for the various situations in life:

- Planting of trees
- Eating bread
- Drinking wine
- Observing a comet
- When it rains
- Moving into a new house
- Wearing new clothes
- Honoring a new king
- (And for Californians, there is a blessing for earthquakes!)

It is common in Jewish homes for the father to pronounce a blessing on his children every day. What would Christian families be like if each member received a spoken blessing every day? Would children grow up more self-confident and aware of parents' love and God's presence? Would there be a more positive spirit in our homes? Many wonder how the Jewish people have survived the atrocities and cruel treatment over the centuries. Could it be that they experienced strength from receiving a personal word of spoken affirmation every day since they were born? I think there is a connection.

Shabbat: Sabbath Celebration _____

I (Tim) was rushing back to the church one Saturday evening for another meeting.

Red light! It seemed to be taking longer than usual. I thought, *I hope this light doesn't make me late for my meeting!*

The sun was beginning to set and cast long shadows from the men in dark clothes and yarmulkes passing in front of me in the crosswalk. On their way to synagogue, they were deep in conversation and smiling, enjoying the reasonable and smooth pace of their day. I was frantic, grinding gears, and stressing about being late to church. Then it occurred to me: they were keeping Sabbath, and I wasn't.

The Lord's Day can be anything but a day of rest. As a culture, we have lost the value of Sabbath. We have made it like every other day. We have forgotten the Fourth Commandment:

Remember the Sabbath day by keeping it holy. Six days you shall labor and do all your work, but the seventh day is a Sabbath to the Lord your God. On it you shall not do any work, neither you, nor your son or daughter, nor your manservant or maidservant, nor your animals, nor the alien within your gates. For in six days the Lord made the heavens and the earth, the sea, and all that is in them, but he rested on the seventh day. Therefore the Lord blessed the Sabbath day and made it holy (Ex. 20:8-11).

. . . . .

Stock Car

When our daughter turned sixteen, we bought a used car and gave her stock in it. She started with ten percent. As she proves her driving skills and responsibility, she will earn another ten percent. We made a stock certificate with ten boxes. As she earns a box, we sign and date it. The plan is, by the time she is eighteen, she will be 100 percent responsible for the car (including the costs!).

Suzanne Smith, Thousand Oaks, CA

. . . . .

Holy.

Special.

Set apart.

Judaism has given the world a gift—awareness that time is sacred. Six days are sufficient to work, according to Scripture. God deserves a day of focus. We deserve a day of rest. We celebrate the sanctity of time when we keep the Sabbath. The rabbis teach that when we keep Sabbath, we become refreshed (Ex. 31:17); we gain endurance for the trials and challenges of the coming week. The ancient Greeks and Romans ridiculed the Jews for being lazy one day every week. The Greek and Roman civilizations have fallen, but the Jewish people are thriving. God's Word is powerful, and when followed, provides a blessing.

Sabbath is not meant to be a dreary, religious ritual; it is to be a time of special foods, relaxing conversation, and focus on God. What might happen on a Sunday if you were to turn off the TV; skip the soccer practice; let the roast beef, potatoes, and carrots cook in the crockpot while you were at church; and focus on praising God? When you come home, light some candles, put on a CD with praise music, pull out some fresh bread and the dinner that has been simmering. Make sure the phone answering machine is on, and shut yourself off from the outside world. As you offer a prayer of thanks to God for the food, ask your children to share what they liked about their lesson at church. Place your hands on each child's head and pray a Scripture blessing:

The Lord bless you and keep you;
> *The Lord make his face shine upon you and be gracious to you;*
> *The Lord turn his face toward you and give you peace*
(Num. 6:24-26).

Take a family walk, and leisurely enjoy each other's company. Later, you can establish a one-hour Quiet Time. Have everyone lie down and read—it is a guaranteed way to get a nap. You are following the fourth commandment—you are resting!

Rosh Hashanah

The celebration of the Jewish New Year is Rosh Hashanah. At a Rosh Hashanah service, participants greet each other with wishes for a prosperous and fulfilling year: "As God puts His final seal on you, may it be for good."[5] Upon returning home, candles are lit and special round bread—in the shape of a wheel, symbolizing connection with time—is broken and dipped in honey. The honey symbolizes a sweet new year. A prayer is offered: "May it be Your will, Lord, our God and God of our fathers, to renew unto us a good and sweet year."

Some Jewish families enjoy a walk to a stream or body of water where they go for *Tashlikh* (prayer). It comes from the word "cast" in Micah 7:19 (KJV) and represents the idea of casting your sins on the water. Jewish families take bread and cast it out into the water as a means of celebrating God's forgiveness.

In our culture, a common way to launch the New Year involves parties and alcohol, leaving no room for a celebration of God and what we hope He will do in the future. Consider adapting your New Year traditions to include verbal blessings for each other, candles, special breads, and a blessing for your children. Try to redeem the holiday and make it spiritually significant.

Sukkot

At harvest time, the Jews celebrate Sukkot and make a festive bouquet called an *Arba Minim,* in which the plants used reflect all the senses. The *Arba Minim* was carried to the synagogue for the festival prayer service in a festive parade of gratefulness to God—the Provider. The rabbis often discussed the elements of the bouquet as desirable qualities of character. The citron resembles the heart and represents emotion. The date palm branch is straight and strong, like a human spine. The willows from the brook stand for lips, instruments of speech. Only by dedicating these organs individually and jointly to the service of God could a faithful Jew expect to become whole. Leo Trepp writes:

The Rabbis extended the symbolism of the four plants to human society. There are persons endowed with kindness and courtesy (smell) and with wisdom (taste), like the citron. Others, like the date, may lack in courtesy (no smell), but are rich in wisdom (taste). Some, like the myrtle, may be filled with kindness (smell) but lack wisdom (no taste). Finally, many will have no distinctions at all, like the willows of the brook. But no single human individual is expendable. If but one is slighted or excluded, the whole of society is patal, unfit.[6]

Christians might adapt a similar idea and make harvest festival bouquets as an expression of gratefulness for God's provision, then meet for a feast to celebrate. "Give thanks in all circumstances, for this is God's will for you in Christ Jesus" (1 Thes. 5:18). We like the idea of using all five senses to declare praise and gratefulness to God. It demonstrates a wholehearted appreciation of the fact that we have been made whole and acceptable by what Christ did for us at the cross. We don't have to earn our salvation. Christ paid for it and ransomed us.

→ Chapter 7 ←

The Art of Tradition

*U*sing family traditions to pass on a heritage is an art, not a science. It requires finesse. Each family must develop its own unique blend based upon personalities, purposes, and habits. This art form cannot be learned by reading a book, or carefully following a five-step program. A cookie-cutter approach won't work. Nor can we copy a formula used effectively by other families, because formulas aren't always transferable. A formula that works remarkably well with one child won't necessarily work well with another. Formulas are limited to the culture, situation, and demographic of a particular environment. They may work in one family, but not in the family next door.

The goal of formulas is to fix behavior: stop "bad" behavior and change it to "good." The problem is, it is possible to alter external behavior with no real learning taking place. Focusing on behavior is appropriate for younger children and in situations where a physical change is required: for example, the child wants to play in the street or touch a hot stove. Formula-based parenting says, "Do it this way and you will get this result." It is simple, predictable, and seems to offer a guarantee. Formula-based parenting does work—but usually just for the short term. When the external pressure of the parent is lifted, the child reverts back to what originally motivated him to misbehave.

When it comes to traditions—do not think formulas, think principles: proven, fundamental truths that have universal application and are transferable from situation to situation, place to place, and family to family. Principle-based parenting seeks to internalize transferable concepts within the child. The focus is on the thinking of the child (not simply his behavior). We are concerned with what motivates a child. We want the child to learn to make wise choices, to be motivated from the inside out. We don't want to be the moral conscience of the child, we want him to develop his own conscience. The results of a principle-based approach seem to be long term. If the child has made an inner commitment to a principle, he tends to stick with it—even when Mom or Dad isn't around! When principles are integrated into a parent's thinking, they begin to shape character. In time, the character shaping produces a desirable habit. Principles help parents become less rigid, less perfectionistic, and more effective.

Principle-centered parenting has three critical components:

. . . . .

Saint Lucia

We dress Anne as St. Lucia and have her make cinnamon rolls that she brings to the whole family and the family next door. We bought the crown (which has battery operated candles) from the American Girls catalog and it is a highlight for her. Saint Lucia was a Roman woman who brought food to the persecuted Christians hiding in the catacombs. She put candles in her hair wreath so she would have her hands free to carry the food. We want to train our daughter to care for others, too.

Lori Davis, Wheaton, IL

. . . . .

1. It is based on proven, timeless principles.
2. It provides long-term focus.
3. It is effective in a variety of situations.

PRINCIPLE : Using traditions is more of an art than a science.

INTENTIONAL IMPACT: I will experiment with traditions using principles, not formulas.

	FORMULAS	PRINCIPLES
Goal:	Fix behavior	Internalize transferable concepts
Focus:	Behavior of the child	Thinking of the child
Learning:	May not take place	Learning usually takes place
Results:	Short term	Long term

Principle-centered parenting is based on the belief that there are certain universal values admirable in all cultures, for all time. The loss of absolutes within our culture has left us with uncertainty and a wimpy relativism. We need a moral compass for our children and ourselves, and values we can believe in. The alternative is to continue what we are doing, and somehow keep ourselves busy so we don't notice that our kids are growing up with an acute sense of entitlement, and a dull sense of responsibility.[1] Principle-centered parenting affirms the existence of absolutes: universal laws that govern relationships just as natural laws govern nature.

The Artful Passing of the Baton

The music was coming from my (Tim) daughter's bedroom: "BOOM-BOOM-BOOM!" The familiar beat brought back a flood of memories—memories I'd hoped would be eternally forgotten (like my photo ID from eighth grade). She turned up the volume. The rhythm drew me in. Before long, I was singing along with Donna Summer. That's right, I'm a recovering disco fanatic. *Could Nicole have a latent disco gene released by hormones at age sixteen?* I wondered. I'm not sure, but one thing I do know: From generation to generation, parents pass down habits, tendencies, traditions, and traits for good and bad. Like you, I want to pass on more than traits of music appreciation to my children. I want to leave them a legacy.

A legacy is an emotional and spiritual inheritance that you pass like a relay baton to your child. As a track-and-field coach for our local club, I train athletes to focus on the essentials. In a relay, passing the baton successfully is essential. When we hand our "batons" to our kids, we want them to grasp with ease and run well. We want to empower our children to continue the race of life knowing we love them and have blessed them. The best legacies equip children to run with confidence and make wise decisions long after they leave home.

Like passing a baton on the track, which requires rhythm and timing, passing on a legacy of traditions requires six basic steps. These steps will impact the future of our children. The greatest legacy a parent can leave a child is a lasting faith in Jesus Christ.

1. Don't compartmentalize your faith.

Some of us relegate spiritual issues to certain times or places. Our kids notice. They might say we're not consistent and call us hypocrites. If they say they believe one way and yet behave another, they might tell us they learned that from their parents.

·····

Grandchild's File

When our grandchildren were born, we purchased a *Time* magazine for the week of their birth, and the front page of the newspaper was saved from the day of their birth. These go in their file, along with other keepsakes. We will mark their spiritual birth and other major events in a similar way.

Scott Owsley, San Jose, CA

·····

Our faith should influence how we manage our money, spend our time, entertain, and relate to others. When our kids see a growing and vital faith touching every aspect of our lives, they're more likely to perceive faith as important to us, and therefore it becomes important to them.

When Nicole made a club volleyball team, we were excited. The excitement quickly turned to anxiety when I discovered how expensive the club fees were. Suzanne suggested we pray that "God provide money we don't know of, if this is His will." We asked the girls to pray with us. I had never prayed about volleyball; it seemed to belong in a separate category altogether. Yet within ten days, we received unanticipated business income that we used for the fees.

2. Model a growing and personal faith.

How we behave throughout the day sends messages to our kids. Once again, the words of youth ministry veteran Dave Veerman confirm what most of us know intuitively: "Studies have consistently shown that children . . . become most like their parents in how they live and where they invest their lives."[2]

Our lives are instructive, whether we intend for them to be or not. The key is to become intentional. Include discussions of faith in everyday conversations. Let your kids see you reading your Bible and Christian books. Impress upon them the importance of weekly worship and why you make an effort to be involved in your church. Speak highly of your church leaders—help your children understand and respect them. On your way home from church, share your own ideas about faith. Our daughters know that I attend a weekly breakfast with other Christian men to pray, hold each other accountable, and talk about our faith.

3. Be authentic.

Kids aren't looking for perfection, but for authenticity. They can sniff a phony. Parents caught up in the performance trap tend to be fatigued, but those who have given up the notion of perfection have more energy to parent with authenticity. They don't have to spend so much of it striving for the unattainable.

Walt Mueller, executive director of the Center for Parent/ Youth Understanding, writes:

> *Realistic parents pave the way for family closeness and build their children's self-esteem by* parenting with grace. *They know that since the beginning of time, God has used imperfect people to carry out his plan, and he will use them as they raise their children in spite of their imperfections.* [3]

This concept of *parenting with grace* is liberating. I don't have to be the perfect parent. Since I'm in need of grace, it's easier to admit when I'm wrong and to ask for forgiveness. It's still not easy, but when I keep in mind what God has done for me, I'm motivated to say: "I overreacted about the kitchen being a mess. Will you forgive me?"

4. Serve together.

If it's true that values are *caught* rather than *taught,* you'll want to spend time throwing values your kids will catch. We met a family who had little materially and invited them for dinner. Nicole and Brooke used their allowance to purchase a toy truck for the boy, then picked a couple of their stuffed animals in good condition for the girls, along with two beautiful handmade dresses they had outgrown. I'll never forget the family's tears of gratitude. Neither will our daughters.

As a family, talk about what you could do together to demonstrate your faith. Tell your kids, "We're going to take our faith on the road. What should we do?" Pick age-appropriate activities that match your family members' gifts and abilities.

5. Pray with and for your kids—and yourself.

I like to tuck our daughters in at night and ask, "What would you like me to pray about?" I let them know I'm praying for their specific requests and check later to see how things are going. If you're like me, you want to pray for your kids, but get busy and forget. Try assigning a *memory minder* to each child. For Nicole and me, it's McDonald's; we've been going there since she was two. It's our special place. Whenever I see the golden arches, I pray for her. Brooke has a daily habit of turning on the Weather Channel and checking out the variables of Southern California weather. My reminder to pray for her is the weather report on the radio or any discussion of the weather that I might hear throughout the day. I quickly utter, "God help Brooke weather her day at middle school!"

We also need to pray for ourselves. We worry about how we're doing, don't we? Prayer offers perspective and helps us deal with anxiety. "Do not be anxious about anything," writes Paul, "but in everything, by prayer and petition, with thanksgiving, present your requests to God" (Phil. 4:6). (Now that our daughters are teenagers, I recite this often!)

. . . . .

Restaurant Wait Entertainment

As you are waiting in the lobby for a table, play, "Who's Next?" Try to guess the age, gender and type of clothing of the next person to enter the door. Another game is "May I Serve You?" If you can see the servers, study how they serve their customers. Ask, "Do they look like they are serving with joy?" "Are they quick, efficient, and thoughtful? Why?" "What do you think they do in their free time?" A third activity, for those really long waits, is "Servant Stories." Take a 3x5 card and pencil with you. See if your children can list times in Scripture when someone served another person. On the back of the card, ask them to record, or draw a picture of, a time when they served someone.

Suzanne Smith, Thousand Oaks, CA

. . . . .

6. Communicate love in your child's language.

If you are going to speak to the natives, you have to learn their language. Each child has a language of love, according to Gary Chapman and Ross Campbell in *The Five Love Languages of Children*[4]. If you can discover and speak your child's love language, you'll be better able to meet her emotional needs and help her develop into a healthy adult. The authors say that a child most likely receives love through one of these five areas: quality time, words of affirmation, gifts, acts of service, physical touch. Brooke's primary love language is quality time with me or her mom. She loves it when I play basketball with her, but doesn't respond to conversations as her sister does. Her secondary love language is physical touch; she warms up after we've played, then sit down for a soda and snuggle. As you discover your child's love language, speak it daily, and don't neglect the four secondary areas.

Prepare for the Handoff _____

PRINCIPLE : Parents have the primary responsibility for the spiritual development of their children.

INTENTIONAL IMPACT: Through the intentional use of events, stories, a family creed, and customs, I will seek to pass on a rich spiritual heritage.

There are four ways to pass on the legacy within your family:
EVENTS: achievements worth memorializing, around which you develop traditions.
STORIES: the culture of family with its values and community spirit passed on through telling.
CREED: a list of foundational beliefs you esteem and uphold.
CUSTOMS: common behaviors that are repeated.

Events

The Jewish people provide a striking example of celebrating events. In the biblical record, Israel realized the importance of current events and memorialized them. Those days became symbolic. Events over the years became a catalyst for generational passing of the heritage. We read about the night in Egypt when the death angel visited and passed over those who placed blood on the doorposts (Passover) . . . the day Esther put her life on the line and faced down Haman to deliver her people from genocide (Purim) . . . the day when the Temple at Jerusalem was destroyed at the hands of Babylonian conquerors and the Jewish people were forced into exile (Tisha B'Av). These events are celebrated, mourned, and remembered with an eye toward their heritage. They dare not allow future generations to overlook such significant events.[5]

What are significant Christian events? In chapter three we introduced the concept of a monument time line:

Time Line

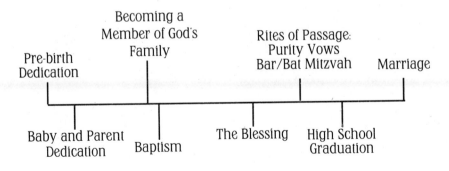

Are there other key spiritual events you would add to this time line? Take a few minutes to capture your initial thoughts about these events and lay the foundation for a tradition celebrating the event. Using the following questions, write some of your rough ideas.

Event
Why do we celebrate this event?

What Scripture is important?

Who should be involved in planning this event?

Is there a theme or atmosphere to capture?

How much will the tradition event vary from individual to individual?

After you have responded to these questions, move on to another traditional event. Record your thoughts on the extra copies beginning on page 199. Record across the time line the themes, symbols, and people who will be a meaningful part of the family's traditions. Themes might be based on a Scripture passage, for instance. For a rite of passage, you might choose 1 Timothy 4:12: "Don't let anyone look down on you because you are young, but set an example for the believers in speech, in life, in love, in faith and in purity" (NIV), and choose "Set a Good Example" as a theme. A symbol is any physical object that conveys meaning, such as a cross or a family heirloom.

Stories

People feel connected when they know the story. Storytelling may be the oldest form of passing legacy. Early on, people entertained each other by telling stories around the fire. Stories define families, communicate values and history, and bond us to one another. Stories can be a fun and influential way to develop meaningful family traditions.

According to James Fowler, Ph.D., a professor of theology and human development at Emory University, at about the age of four:

> *a natural metaphysical interest awakens and there are various ways for parents to cultivate that. Most important are gifts to the imagination of the child. These come in the tactile richness of*

. . . . .

Mornings

When I drop my children off at school in the morning, I make the sign of the cross on their foreheads and give them a blessing, such as: "Go with God, serve Him well," or "Remember, you belong to God." I do this because as I am sending them into the world for the day—and heading to work myself—I want them to remember their true center point. Recently, my son has been reciprocating the action by giving me the sign of the cross and speaking a blessing to me!

Susan Miller, Colorado Springs, CO

. . . . .

rituals (at home or at church): the smell of incense, the lighting of candles, the singing of hymns, the telling of stories.[6]

Wisdom and values are embedded in story. In fact, stories have more impact on young children than moral teachings on right and wrong. Preschool children often have an acute sense of shame, feeling easily shamed by a moralistic teaching. But a story is illustrative—it guides them into proper behavior, drawing a picture of virtue in action without triggering shame. As children reach six to nine years old, they become more comfortable with storytelling than preschoolers because they are less ego-centered. They begin to understand basic moral behavior, such as the principle of reciprocity or the Golden Rule: "I treat others like I would like to be treated."

"Stories become a powerful foundation for children to gain a sense of their history within a religious or spiritual community,"[7] according to Nina Jaffe, a folklore specialist, author, and professor.

It is common in West African tradition for children to become part of the story. They are invited to interrupt the storyteller at certain points by saying, "I was there," to which the storyteller responds, "What did you see?" You might use this method if you were telling children about the resurrection of Christ, for example. You could pause and encourage them to say, "I was there."

"What did you see?"

"I saw a big rock in front of a huge cave."

"What else?"

"I saw a giant angel standing in front of the cave."

"What was going on?"

"People were scared 'cuz Jesus was lost. He's supposed to be in that cave."

The value of making stories interactive is that it engages the imagination of the child. As children hear the story, they interact with the story line—which means they are personalizing abstract concepts like courage, good sense, or caution. Consider telling stories this way to engage your child's imagination and involvement. Remember that the point isn't to finish the story, but to stimulate your child's creative process around desirable virtues. Remember, with children, it's process over product. The value is in the process, not getting the task done.

Creed

Reconsider the definition of tradition: *the practice of handing down stories, beliefs, and customs from one generation to another in order to establish and reinforce a strong sense of identity.* Perhaps the most important aspect of giving a strong sense of identity is passing a clear, credible belief system from one generation to the next. One way of doing so is to establish a family creed—a list of foundational beliefs you will esteem and uphold.

In our pluralistic culture many parents recoil at this idea. They feel that it is too restrictive, maybe even manipulative. They subscribe to a "let kids decide for themselves" mentality, in which children grow up in a spiritual vacuum, and are expected to make decisions about spiritual matters without spiritual experience or skills. This may be the only area in life where parents expect their children to make critical decisions without any preparation or assistance. The "hands-off" approach doesn't make sense.

We are not saying a parent should force beliefs on children. Each individual has a right to choose. But as loving parents we have a responsibility to help our children mature spiritually. Consider these words from *The Heritage*:

> *Protecting a child's freedom to choose is one thing.*
> *Withholding our parental influence is another. It is imperative that parents drive their stake in the ground—that they intentionally train and mentor their children in the tenets of their*

faith. Passive silence is not a sign of open-mindedness. It is rather a sign of negligence.[8]

Children have a natural curiosity for spiritual issues. To help them mature and develop, we need to address this built-in inquiry rather than say, "figure it out when you are older." That merely gives the child the impression we don't care about spiritual issues, or aren't capable of discussing them.

Phil Catalfo, author of *Raising Spiritual Children in a Material World: Introducing Spirituality Into Family Life,* has strayed from his Catholic roots, but is seeing the need to address the spiritual hunger of his children. His book is a result of this quest. He writes:

Among other things, parents are spiritual gardeners, and it falls to us to cultivate the ground in which our children's spiritual beliefs take root . . . it seems that our reluctance to force-feed our children any religion translated into no feeding at all.[9]

I find it interesting that a book from a secular publisher critiques our culture's *laissez-faire* approach to children's spirituality. Even from a secular perspective the mandate is clear: *Parents have the responsibility to contribute to the spiritual development of their children.* How much more important from a Christian perspective to establish a family creed.

How to develop your family creed

1. *Recognize your creed.* Discuss what you believe and why, including your values, truth, virtues, God, the church, family, personal character, human nature, and eternal destiny.

2. *Refine your creed.* Compare and contrast your values as family members. Seek to clarify confusion or disagreements. Try to develop something you all agree on.

3. *Record your creed.* Put it in writing. Display it in a prominent place. Allow it to influence your thought patterns and decisions.

4. *Reference your creed.* Refer to it often. Talk about it when you get up, when you walk, and when you go to bed. Allow your creed to influence every aspect of your life.

Many businesses are gaining clarity and motivation with a mission statement. It is a purpose-oriented statement that defines what the organization is about and what it is called to do. Some individuals have adapted this concept to a personal mission statement. A family creed is similar to a family mission statement, but has several distinctives.

A FAMILY MISSION STATEMENT	A FAMILY CREED
Represents what is important to you.	Represents what is important to God and you.
Focuses on unique talents of the individual.	Sees individual talent as God's gift to benefit others.
Is based on what we can do as a family.	Says what we can do as a family with God's help.
Is oriented to the present.	Considers our connection with the past and future.
	Accepts responsibility to pass on a heritage.
	Sees a connection to the family of God.
	Includes the spiritual dimension.
	Is inspirational, based on God's Word and Spirit.

A sample family creed: *Our family exists to help each member grow to his or her full God-given potential. We believe that we can enjoy a life of meaning and fun, and we seek to pass the abundant life on to others.*

Begin to develop a family creed for your family. Use the following worksheet.

Family Creed Worksheet

1. What is important to you?

2. What is important to God? (List Scripture verses.)

3. What gifts and talents has God given our family members?

4. How can these be used to contribute to others?

5. What is our family's potential? With God's help, what could we do to serve Him?

6. What are some key strengths from our family history?

7. What are some key weaknesses from our family history?

8. How can we use our strengths and weaknesses to benefit us now, and in the future?

9.What steps can we take to pass on a godly and healthy heritage?

10. What have we done to strengthen our connection with God's family? What could we do?

11. What seems to be working to help us grow spiritually strong?

12. What Scripture has a special history for our family? How have we seen God's Word become a reality in our family life?

13. How has God's Spirit empowered our family? How have we seen God's power in our family?

Customs

Customs are common behaviors that are repeated. They don't need to be elaborate. In fact, the most influential customs tend to be simple, easy to overlook, and may not be considered forms of tradition. But like every discipline, the art of creating traditions requires basic skills. These are elementary, but can't be overlooked. Like learning to drive, skydive, or surf, ignoring the basics could lead to injury. We need to learn the fundamentals if we are going to improve our skills. We need the discipline of the smaller stuff to lay the foundation for the bigger stuff. Customs are the baby steps in the art of tradition. The following ten customs aren't exciting, but they are the nuts and bolts of developing skills in the art of tradition. Without these ten, or similar ones tailored for your family, as a foundation, other more complex customs may fall flat.

1. When you begin the day, greet people in your family before you ask something from them.

2. Establish a positive environment with pleasant music instead of the TV news.

3. Sit down as a family for breakfast, and ask God's blessing on the food and the day ahead.

4. As the children leave for school, offer a quick verbal prayer, "God, give Jamie a super day at school."

5. Listen to Christian music or radio on your drive to work or school.

6. Page, voice mail, or e-mail each other during the day just to say, "I love you."

7. Do "Favorites Friday." Bring home everyone's favorite gum, candy, soda, juice, snack, or fruit.

8. Help someone finish a chore once in a while—people are more important than task.

9. Don't leave personal belongings in the car, living room, or other shared living spaces.

10. Take time to say good night to each family member, and pray with children as you tuck them in.

Finish Well

One of the worst things that can happen in a relay is to drop the baton. To avoid this, track-and-field teams practice handing it off. They work on stride, rhythm, signals, and movement. In a way, it's a dance. Some teams have faster runners, but drop the baton and end up losing the race to slow and steady runners who know how to pass on the baton and finish well.

Life with kids is a relay. Societies are influenced one family at a time. The family is God's primary institution for passing on the truth of His Word from one generation to the next. The implication is clear: When parents drop the baton of godly legacy, the nation suffers. And yet, if we commit ourselves to be intentional about passing the baton, we'll give our children an inheritance they can't outspend, and a heritage that will outlive us. We will have impressed upon their hearts and minds a love for God and an unshakable faith in Him. Such gifts are rare, but priceless.

⚘ Chapter 8 ⚘

Begin with
the End in Mind

⟨⟨⟨⟨⟨⟩⟩⟩⟩⟩

I (Tim) got nervous when our older daughter turned twelve. I set out to research the critical issues facing young adolescents. Surveying over five hundred junior-high-school-age students, I selected thirty topics that expressed their most common concerns. *Okay, I'll lecture her on these,* I thought. Then I remembered my own advice to parents of teens: "Not every moment is a teachable moment."

What should I do? I knew that many parents back off parenting when their child reaches adolescence. That may be the time they need us the most, but in a different way.

I decided to study what might work best with *Nicole.* I knew what worked with her probably would not work with her sister, Brooke. I knew I had to customize a personal connection with Nicole to be successful in dealing with the thirty topics. The clock was ticking. The hormones were beginning to kick in. I wanted to develop a plan.

Then it hit me—*McDonald's!* We enjoyed "Daddy-Daughter Time" at Playland and occasionally I'd sneak a few trips down the purple, swirly slide. (Hey, after thousands of dollars of cheeseburgers, I earned them!) We had always talked at

McDonald's, so why not talk there now—about the thirty topics? Unsure how to organize the discussions, I remembered Nicole loves to get mail. I thought, *I will write her letters!*

I took my list of thirty topics and began writing my daughter letters about life. I pictured various teens in my ministry who reflected character qualities I wanted to see develop in Nicole. Her mother and I had talked about many of these. Now it was critical to become intentional about them. I set out to write letters that would help Nicole navigate the teen years and develop these desirable qualities.

Nicole and I met once or twice a month for the year preceding her thirteenth birthday. We munched on Big Macs, she read my letters, then we talked about . . .

- emotions and expectations
- her changing body and true beauty
- strategies to deal with temptation
- setting sexual standards

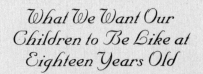

What We Want Our Children to Be Like at Eighteen Years Old

Spiritual
To have a growing and vibrant faith in Christ

Social
To be able to make wise choices about friends and activities
To be able to relate to a wide variety of people in diverse situations

Physical
To be in good health and maintain habits of an active lifestyle
To preserve their virginity until they are married
To live a substance-abuse-free lifestyle

Emotional
To feel capable, confident of self, and God-given abilities
To draw boundaries (not be taken advantage of by others—personal courage)

Mental
To be prepared for opportunities encountered in the future
To think critically and biblically (Christian worldview)

Character
To be honest, just, dependable, forgiving, compassionate, generous

Life Skills
To develop skills in finances, vocational planning, ministry involvement, cooking, cleaning, car maintenance, and personal organization

- relating to and dating non-Christians
- using alcohol, drugs, and tobacco
- school, pain, and death
- popularity versus character

There isn't a topic I *haven't* discussed with Nicole. I think these discussions have paid off. They demonstrated to her that she was important enough to me that I would design a meaningful way to discuss important issues.

Writing letters to teenagers isn't an original idea. When I was a teen, I read and reread Charlie Shedd's *Letters To Karen*—a father's letters to his daughter prior to her wedding. But nowadays we can't wait until our children are about to get married to deal with some of these issues. We need to begin discussing them while our kids are still young.

. . . . .

Dinner Debrief

At dinner every night we play the "Best Part of the Day." Someone says, "Best Part of the Day" and every hand goes up. The last hand is the one who shares the best part of his or her day, then calls out "Best Part of the Day" and so on, until all family members are finished sharing.

David Olshine, Columbia, SC

. . . . .

Developing a Blueprint _____

Recently, a team of pastors met with a contractor to review blueprints for the construction of a new church building. Anticipation filled the air. They studied the blueprints to see how the plans would accommodate hundreds of children and youth, as well as adults involved in ministry. Then the project foreman asked, "What do you think about the blueprint? Where would you like to be three years from now? How do you expect to grow?" These were challenging questions.

We apply the same questions to parenting. We aren't constructing buildings. We are building lives. Do you have a blueprint? Where would you like to be three years from now? What do you want your kids to look like when you are finished parenting? How do you expect to help them get there?

I like what Becky Tirabassi writes about blueprints:

With the excitement and anticipation of a new building project, an architect and a contractor sit with a client, assuring him of successful completion of the project by displaying blueprints, pictures and sketches of similar completed buildings. They explain flowcharts of dates for breaking ground, erecting steel, pouring concrete, and doing finish work, detailing all the components of the building, though not yet begun. Similarly, time spent with God in conversation regarding dreams and hopes creates a form and plan for the desires of one's heart, proposing that in God's timing and by His blueprint they will come to pass.[1]

Have you talked with God about your plans and desires for your children? Have you submitted your plans to the Master Architect for His approval? A parent demonstrates faith when willing to submit highest hopes to Him. Obeying God in the unseen areas means allowing Him to have influence over your dreams—dreams for yourself and your children. "Now faith is being sure of what we hope for and certain of what we do not see" (Heb. 11:1). You have the opportunity to build your family's faith on a foundation of prayer, a faith-building exercise. Prayer helps us imagine our children's future with confidence because we know that they won't walk alone—God will be with them. Faith cannot be manufactured or manipulated. It is a response from within us, orchestrated by God. It is His supernatural work within us that generates our ability to trust Him with our lives, and our children's lives.

Have you recorded in writing your hopes for your children?

Tim Kimmel writes:

It takes a lot more than good intentions to leave a legacy of love. The best intentions have a tough time competing with the relentless pressures of culture. We have to be focused and strategic. Good intentions that aren't followed by specific actions are just empty words.[2]

The point is, raising kids who turn out right demands that we have a clear idea of what's required. Developing a blueprint for the finished product puts us miles ahead. Obvious benefits come from knowing in advance the kind of adults we want to create out of the raw materials that live under our roofs. Anxiety is often the result of confusion. People can't figure out who they are, what they are trying to accomplish, or where they are heading. . . . By having a strategy for developing our children's character, we release our spirits from the bondage of fear. We can rest in the fact that we see the big picture—even while we struggle with the day-to-day challenges that come from overseeing a family. [3]

Anxiety is the result of confusion? Yes, as parents, many times we don't have a clear idea of how to parent our child. When something unexpected happens, we stop leading and begin responding. We respond to the culture, the environment, the emotion of the moment. But hopefully, we want to be influencers, not reactors. To move into that position, we need to develop clear goals. What kind of people do we want our children to become? With what character qualities? Which life skills?

It's like heading out on a family vacation. We need to have a destination, do some planning, and expect it to be a positive experience. Can you imagine saying, "C'mon, let's go! Grab your suitcase, get in the car"?

"Where are we going, Daddy?" asks the youngest from the backseat.

"On a family vacation; that's all I know!"

Disaster.

When vacationing, or raising a child, begin with the end in mind.

We will enjoy parenting more if we have a blueprint and make intentional steps to parent accordingly. Develop a plan, and communicate it to your children. They will feel more secure, be more inclined to cooperate, and their confidence in your leadership will grow.

PRINCIPLE : Parenting requires a plan.

INTENTIONAL IMPACT: I will develop a blueprint for each child. I need a plan that works, and then I need to work the plan.

. . . . .

Travel Tips

When we travel out of town, we leave an audiotape of a prayer and a good-night song for each day for our children. We also leave a book with a letter for each day written on its own page. The letter is written on half of the page and the page is folded over so that the letter is concealed. The open sides are bound together so that the letter can't be read until the folded edge is cut. These provide daily contact with us, and a place for our children to record notes to us to read when we return.

Lori Davis, Wheaton, IL

. . . . .

What Is Your Target?

You need to have a target for your kids. No, we didn't say, "use your kids as a target!" (Even though there are days you would like to.) What bull's-eye are you aiming for as you raise your children? How will you know if you have hit it? The psalmist compared children to arrows.

> *Sons are a heritage from the Lord, children a reward from him.*
> *Like arrows in the hands of a warrior are sons born in one's*

youth. Blessed is the man whose quiver is full of them
(Ps. 127:3-5).

If children are like arrows, they need to be pointed in the right direction. Our culture feels the impact of children who have not been pointed toward the target of learning personal responsibility and compassion. There are children who shoot and kill other children. They are like arrows without direction.

An un-aimed arrow is a dangerous thing. But our culture is full of two kinds of children with problems: those who haven't been aimed, and those who haven't been released. Our role as parent archers is to aim our children toward the bull's-eye and then release. If we do not release, it will have the same result as not aiming—we will miss the target.

Let go.

I know that is difficult for protective parents. Letting go feels like being irresponsible. You ask:

"What if my children make poor choices?"

"What if they don't go the distance?"

"What happens if a wind comes along and blows them off course?"

"What if they go too far and high and go over the target?"

There are dozens of things that could go wrong (and you have thought about them often). But you have to let go. You can't run alongside, maintaining contact, if you expect your child to fly.

.....

Christmas Wish Ornaments

I ask family and friends to write a Christmas wish on a piece of paper. I then make ornaments out of each "wish" and hang them on the Christmas tree. The only stipulation is that the "wish" be for something other than material things.

Martha Bolton, Simi Valley, CA

.....

Can you imagine a parent setting up a target, walking back to the marker, drawing the bow with his arrow/child, aiming at the target, pointing the tip of the arrowhead dead center into the red bull's-eye, then releasing the arrow, only to run beside it and guide it with a touch here, a nudge there? Ridiculous, isn't it? Impossible, too. Aim, then release.

The most quoted and most misunderstood Bible verse about parenting is this:

Train a child in the way he should go, and when he is old he will not turn from it (Prov. 22:6).

Some parents wince at the idea of "training" their child. It reminds them of training their puppy, or making a horse jump over barriers. Others may react because it reminds them of boot camp. The word *training* suffers from a lack of positive PR. But used in Scripture, the term means something quite different. The Hebrew word *chanak* could mean at least three different things, depending on the context:

To restrict: enforcing rules, setting guidelines and limits for the child's protection.

To train: as to prepare for battle with conditioning and skill building.

To dedicate: set apart for God's service.

I prefer the third definition and believe it is the most accurate interpretation of the word *chanak* for this particular context. *Chanak* is the root word of the word *Chanukah* or *Hanukkah*, which means "initiation" or "dedication." We are to initiate our children to the Word of God and dedicate them to a life of serving Him, then let them go. Consider Wes Haystead's words:

The rites of dedication declared that the object or place or person was special, out of the ordinary, set apart for God's service. Taken in this sense, the proverb is telling parents to make a conscious, even public commitment that their child belongs to God and will be raised with that special status in mind.

This dedication process goes beyond a one-time ceremony in infancy. Training in this sense involves a continuing aware-ness of the goal that decisions involving the child are not the private prerogative of the parents or the child, but are an acknowledgment that God's purpose must always be primary.[4]

The life of Samuel provides a powerful illustration. After years of praying and asking God to provide a child, Elkanah and Hannah were blessed with the birth of Samuel. Hannah weaned Samuel and traveled to the temple to present him to Eli, the priest. She says, "I prayed for this child, and the Lord has granted me what I asked of him. So now I give him to the Lord. For his whole life he will be given over to the Lord" (1 Sam. 1:27-28).

Hannah understood the concept of *chanak*. She was training Samuel by dedicat-ing him to a life of service to the Lord. It involved an acute awareness of priorities.

> **. . . . .**
>
> ## *Advent Wreath*
>
> During Advent, we use an Advent wreath and light the candles every night, rather than just on Sundays. I look for passages that the children can understand (or we can explain) related to Advent themes, not Christmas. We sing a hymn related to Advent. A week or so before Christmas, we sing carols.
>
> *Susan Miller, Colorado Springs, CO*
>
> **. . . . .**

It involved a huge sacrifice. Knowing that God's purpose was primary, she was willing to give up what she had longed for in order to please her Lord. By doing this, she was modeling for her son *that God's way comes first.* It had an impact on Samuel. In spite of growing up in the temple, he was faced with choices to do evil. Eli's sons were greedy and driven by lust. Samuel chose to go a different way. I believe it was due to the early influence of his godly mother. The aiming of the arrow helped Samuel hit the target.

And the boy Samuel continued to grow in stature and in favor with the Lord and with men (1 Sam. 2:26).

The Way He Should Go _____

Some parents interpret "the way he should go" as one particular right way, a narrow path that all follow to righteousness. They reason, if we can keep our kid on *the path*, everything will eventually turn out right. I don't believe this is what the phrase means. "The way he should go" refers to the natural and unique bent of the shaft of the arrow, another archery term. The goal is for each arrow to hit the target. But some parents, confused, believe the goal is to *shoot each arrow the same*, assuming their children are all alike. This is a fundamental mistake. Each of our children is different, with his or her God-given bent. Tim Kimmel writes,

> *"In the way he should go . . . " literally means "according to his inner bent." The expression has its roots in the idea of a bent bow ready to shoot an arrow. A tailor-made blueprint for each of my children forces me to discover their inner bents, to study the unique qualities and characteristics that make each of them an individual of great potential. Knowing this clarifies my purpose as a parent. It keeps me from being badgered by worldly philosophies.[5]*

An expert archer will pull an arrow from his quiver and stare down the shaft, noticing the slight bend that comes with the wood's natural grain. He will then lay the arrow on the bow, making accommodations for the wind, distance, and location of the target. He will position each arrow differently, depending on its bent. One arrow, he may have tilted slightly up; another, he may have pointed slightly down. If the wind is coming from one side, he may choose to compensate by positioning the arrow with a slight pitch. He will aim (train) his arrow on his target. He will make allowances for the differences in arrows;

each needs to be aimed a bit differently.

"The way he should go" doesn't mean to follow a pre-scribed path. It isn't a formula that, if followed, will produce a godly adult. Many parents focus on their shooting technique, believing they must be *consistent* and follow *the right way* if they can expect to be successful. They are concentrating on pulling back the bowstring, but have forgotten to sight-in their target. Parents who always try to parent *the right way* might be frustrated when a child veers off course. This happens because the parent archer hasn't considered the natural bent of the arrow and made appropriate adjustments. He has focused only on the bow—not the arrow, nor the target. If we are going to successfully hit the target, we need to consider that we are the bow, the arrow is the uniqueness of the child, and the target is what we want to see in our child.

Focus on the Bull's-Eye

Four key areas make up the bull's-eye; this is what we shoot for so that when our children move out from our authority, they have what they need.

To make wise decisions:
In physical issues—diet, exercise, rest, and health
In social issues—choosing friends, dating relationships, resolving conflict
In spiritual issues—maintaining intimacy with God, wor-shiping, staying connected with other Christians, living out faith
In mental issues—critical thinking ability, a developed Christian worldview

To possess character:

Integrity—being the same at church/school/home/work/play

Faith—being positive and confident that God is at work

Self-control—able to resist temptation and avoid destructive habits

Purity—maintaining high standards mentally and sexually

Honesty—being committed to truth

Reliability—keeping his/her word and being dependable

Courage—standing up for personal convictions and doing what is right

To have vision and purpose:

Vision—a clear mental picture of who she/he wants to be and what she/he wants to do

Purpose—maintaining commitment to do something significant for the benefit of others and the glory of God

To have and use critical life skills:

At home—cook, drive, sew, iron, care for clothes, house cleaning and maintenance, shopping and planning a menu

Personal skills—living on a budget, managing a checkbook, tithing, using credit wisely (avoiding debt), saving, personal organization, time management

Interpersonal skills—reconciliation, setting boundaries, forgiveness, poise, manners, conversation

As you look through this list, you will see several specific goals. Make these specific and personalize them to your child. Customize the target for each of your children, using the following chart to prepare a bull's-eye for each. For instance, for life skills, you might want to write: *Personal responsibility means that he takes good care of his belongings.*

(You'll find additional copies of the chart on page 205.)

Target: A Mature and Prepared Young Adult

The four skill areas my children need to begin life on their own.

To make wise decisions:

To possess character:

To have vision and purpose:

To have and use life skills:

Beginning with the End in Mind

"How did you learn to shoot so good?"
The boy asked his dad, as they entered the wood.
"Watch closely, Son, and you will find,
That you must begin with the end in mind."

"First, pick a branch—straight and strong.
Just the right breadth, and not too long.
You chip off the bark and whittle and hone
'Til the bow is right, but not yet done."

"Your mother twists and spins fine yarn.
She gathers beeswax out by the barn.
Prepares the bowstring with earnest care,
That'll shoot the arrows straight in the air."

"Ah, yes, the arrows—each is unique.
Chosen and fashioned, its own mark to seek.

Each one is different in bent and hue,
When placed on the bow with target in view."

"The bow is raised, the string drawn tight,
The arrow streaks into glorious flight.
Howling winds demand it to veer,
But the archer's aim is pure and clear."

"You ask me, Son, 'But where will it land?'
Well, that depends on the archer's hand.
He is the one whom all things designed,
Because he began with the end in mind."

Doug Thompson

→ *Chapter 9* ←

Challenges to Tradition

don't want to do Family Night tonight! It's stupid!"
"Honey, it is what we do. We have been doing it for
years. Why the hassle now?"

"It's so boring. The little kids like it, but I've outgrown it. It's
for babies!"

This scenario could happen in your family. Let's say you
have worked on your blueprint for your children, maintaining
Family Night for several years, and you were just beginning to
think about a rite of passage for your twelve year old when he
dumps this reaction on you. What should you do when your
child rejects your family traditions?

Let's go back to the definition of a tradition: *the practice of
handing down stories, beliefs, and customs, from one generation to
another, in order to establish and reinforce a strong sense of identity.*

Your goal is to pass on values, and strengthen identity and
community. Family traditions are God-given vehicles to pass on
a strong heritage. They are the tools we use to pass on an emotional, spiritual, and social inheritance. Traditions are a means
to an end, but they aren't the end itself. If traditions are tools,
there are a variety of ways to use them. If your child resists a

tradition it may be time to evaluate things.

Is it time to modify the tradition to a more age-appropriate variation?

Is something going on with that particular child you need to look into?

A hammer has several purposes—to pound nails, separate boards that are nailed together, and pound a stake into the ground. But if there are no nails, that doesn't mean you should throw out the hammer. Just because a child challenges traditions doesn't mean it's time to throw out the tradition. It may be simply a signal to look deeper into the life of the child or consider adapting the tradition. Sometimes the change may be minor and stylistic. Other times it may require a dramatic shift. Just because we change how we use the tool doesn't mean it is any less valuable. Don't get stuck in the rut of maintaining a tradition that may have lost its effectiveness.

> . . . . .
>
> ## New Year's Eve Kid Party
>
> We set the clocks way ahead and have a celebration with the kids when the clock strikes twelve. We pass around soda in fancy cups, finger foods, kisses, and hugs. We give each other awards for achievements that year. These are made from wide gold ribbon and silver seal stickers (available at office supply stores). Past awards included: learned to read, made a friend, wrote my will, helped my parents through a trying time.
>
> *Lori Davis, Wheaton, IL*
>
> . . . . .

A Fresh Perspective

PRINCIPLE: It is reasonable to expect resistance and challenges from children toward family traditions.

INTENTIONAL IMPACT: I will make an effort to keep our family traditions fresh and moving forward.

At the annual 1870 conference of the Indiana Methodist churches, the delegates heard a speech by the president of the college where they were meeting. He said he believed that the world was soon coming into an exciting time of great inventions—among other things, he believed men would someday fly through the air like birds.

The presiding Methodist bishop didn't think much of this. He called it heresy, saying in the Bible, flight is reserved for angels. "There will be no such talk here," he told the delegation. At home, around the dinner table, he told his family what a ridiculous thing the president had spoken of, to believe men will someday fly! The bishop's two young sons, Wilbur and Orville, took it all in, and eventually thought about it from a different perspective. Of course, you know the rest of the story!

No eye has seen, no ear has heard, no mind has conceived what God has prepared for those who love him (1 Cor. 2:9).

We can't imagine what God has in store for our children. Because He is at work, we need to be dynamic, not static. The Greek word to describe the Holy Spirit is from the same root word as the English word *dynamite.* Consider some change to your traditions if warranted. Traditions can become dull rituals if we aren't open to God's involvement. He may have plans we cannot see.

Remember this rule of thumb: *When evaluating traditions— some are keepers, some aren't.*

The parable of the wineskins comes to mind. Jesus was questioned about dealing with change. It seems His disciples had modified the tradition of fasting. When the strict legalists, the Pharisees, had a problem with this, Jesus responded with a parable:

No one sews a patch of unshrunk cloth on an old garment, for the patch will pull away from the garment, making the tear worse. Neither do men pour new wine into old wineskins. If they do, the skins will burst, the wine will run out and the wineskins will be ruined. No, they pour new wine into new wineskins, and both are preserved (Matt. 9:16-17).

While traveling in the desert, people in Bible times carried wine pouches made of animal skins. In the wear and tear of the journey, the skin might get a hole in it. Because new wine expands as it ferments, patching the hole would cause it to leak. New wine would need to be kept in pliable wineskins because old wineskins, unable to expand, burst when filled with new wine. Old wine could be stored in old wineskins because it had stopped fermenting and expanding. New wine required new wineskins. The goal was to preserve both—the old and the new.

. . . . .

Breakfast in Bed

For Mother's Day and Father's Day, the children would make us breakfast in bed. I can't tell you how many times orange juice got spilled, but it was very special!

Claudia Davis, Carmichael, CA

. . . . .

We may not need to *practice* all of the old traditions in our homes, but we want to preserve them. Sometimes, a variation of the container is all that is needed to preserve the tradition.

We (Tim) celebrated our daughters' birthdays with custom parties. When they approached their teen years, they asked us to consider varying our tradition of inviting only one guest per year of age.

"Mom, I can't just invite fourteen friends!" Brooke said. "I have more than that; besides I want to invite boys."

BOYS! It sends a chill down the spine of any father of any daughter. Inviting the opposite gender to your party is a kind of rite of passage, but it still is a reluctant rite of passage for many a parent. Suzanne and I caved in—er, I mean we were *flexible*. It turns out, less than fourteen guests came, but we indicated we wanted to make allowances for age while maintaining some semblance of the tradition.

Children mature in predictable patterns as they develop through stages. We can foresee the patterns, but not the timing of the stages. Don't worry if your child's pace of development is faster or slower than others her age. Each child has a unique internal timetable.

John and Carol Dettoni offer some comforting advice to busy parents in their book *Parenting Before & After Work:*

> *The parent's responsibility is to help, to facilitate, to channel, and to instruct their children as they grow. Parents should not try to control or manipulate or, worse yet, speed up that process of development. All too often parents seek to find ways to make their children into little adults as quickly as possible. This is a common fault that compares to the home gardener who over-waters and over-fertilizes his plants. The result of such anxiousness to get bigger and faster-growing plants is just the opposite: the plants either rot and die or have lots of green leaves and no fruit! Parents should not push for growth, but work with the growth process.[1]*

PRINCIPLE : A tradition may need to be changed in order to preserve the value we are seeking to pass on.

INTENTIONAL IMPACT: Our family will need to adapt certain traditions to make them meaningful and age appropriate.

Responding to a Challenge _____

Some parents are disillusioned when their child challenges a family tradition. They may feel they have failed, or that their child is on the road to delinquency. But challenging traditions is a normal part of the maturing process. As children become individuals, they challenge the familiar. They seek to become who they are—apart from parents. Psychologists call this process "individuation," a normal and natural process of childhood.

When there is conflict regarding a tradition in your family, consider not doing some things. Here are the don'ts:

1. Don't overreact: Our children have a way of pushing our buttons. Sometimes I think they do this just for fun—kind of a sadistic recreational hobby. We may become quickly sucked into the intensity of an argument and explode. We are warned in Scripture to be "quick to listen, slow to speak and slow to become angry" (James 1:19).

2. Don't jump to conclusions: Some parents get most of their exercise this way. We are better off to follow the advice of Proverbs 29:20: "Do you see a man who speaks in haste? There is more hope for a fool than for him."

3. Don't be hurtful: Don't shame your children by degrading them. Focus on the issue—why they don't like the tradition—not on them personally.

Do these things:

1. Listen carefully: Really try to hear what your child is saying. Choose a time when you won't be distracted or rushed.

2. Use the Golden Rule: Jesus commanded that we treat others the way we want to be treated (Luke 6:31). Ask yourself, If I were his age, would I feel the same way he does?

3. Define and discuss the issues:[2] What exactly does your child not like about the tradition? Take time to describe the problem specifically and objectively. Record the issues in writing. Seek first to understand, rather than be understood. Use the following chart.

Tradition Challenge

Our Family Tradition	Value	Evaluation	Alternatives
Thanksgiving at Grandma's	Family togetherness	"Boring"	1. Bring video games 2. Have at our house 3. Rent a cabin

With this chart, you can define and discuss your child's challenge to your tradition. Sometimes just the process of discussing the tradition and emphasizing "why we do this" is helpful enough for the child to understand and accept the tradition.

4. *Emphasize why you have a tradition:* Don't assume that your child understands the value you are trying to teach by your family tradition. You may have to remind her from time to time why you have a certain tradition. Make sure she understands the value you are seeking to teach.

5. *Consider possible alternatives:* Older children (ten and up) need to develop healthy conflict resolution and critical thinking skills. These will pay off later in life when the stakes are high and they need to make wise decisions. If their attitude isn't too belligerent, see if they can recommend some creative alternatives. Be willing to compromise on the form of the tradition, but not the value.

6. *Discuss the alternative tradition with other family members at a family meeting:* Everyone needs to hear the proposed change at the same time. Every family member should have an opportunity to offer an opinion. Consider how the change will impact each family member.

7. *Decide if you want to try the alternative tradition:* You might

> . . . . .
>
> ## *Valentine's Day Roses*
>
> My husband always gives me flowers. It is a tradition carried over from when we were dating. Back then, he would send me a rose for every month that we had been dating. On our eight-month anniversary, he'd send me eight roses, ten-month anniversary, ten roses, and so on. By the time we reached thirty-six roses, we got engaged. I guess he figured it'd be cheaper to marry me!
>
> *Martha Bolton, Simi Valley, CA*
>
> . . . . .

consider doing it on a trial basis. It may create more conflict than the old tradition, or it may breathe new life into a tradition that was beginning to lose its zest (remember new wine requires new wineskins).

Don't be afraid of a challenge to the family tradition, especially if it isn't expressed with disdain.

There is conflict in all relationships at home and church. Parents have a great impact on the values and perspectives of preteen and teenage children in spite of the voices from our culture that deny it. Don't automatically assume that your child's challenge to your tradition has no merit. Their challenge might make it more meaningful. The key is—how do you respond?

In the early church there was a dispute. According to Acts, chapter fifteen, the conflict was resolved by calling a council. Instead of ignoring the issue or forcing it, early Christians discussed it and sought counsel. I believe this is the biblical pattern for resolving conflict. As parents, we can follow this model when our children challenge traditions. If we don't talk with them, we dismiss them and their opinion, "canceling" them. They feel devalued and resentful. We will have exasperated them, something Scripture tells us not to do (Eph. 6:4). When there is conflict over a family tradition, we have two choices, *cancel* or *counsel.* John and Carol Dettoni write,

> Youth also needed to be integrated into their families in ways appropriate for their new developmental achievements in physical, cognitive, social, moral, and spiritual development. Parents can do this by including them in "parental discussions" about major changes coming the family's way [as in changing family traditions]. This allows the young person to make significant and meaningful contributions to the family. Be sure to thank them when they have done so, and give them a direct voice in decisions that affect them—to the degree that you can follow these decisions. Show that the family needs the

young persons in it, that these youth are not a bother or a pain but are loved, accepted, wanted and needed as part of the family.[3]

Milestones of Faith

Children mature through passages on their faith journey. Develop meaningful milestones and traditions that affirm faith and are age appropriate. If you do this, it may reduce the likelihood of your children rejecting a tradition.

AGE	FOCUS	MILESTONE
Infancy	Love	Caress and care for your baby.
Toddler	Prayer	Model prayer for your child.
Preschooler	Sunday School	Discuss and participate with your child.
Early Elementary	Worship	Model, worship together, then discuss.
Middle Elementary	Their Own Bible	Memorize books, read stories together.
Later Elementary	First Communion	Model personal commitment to Christ, baptism.
Middle School	Confirmation or Bar Mitzvah	Accepted into the community of faith.
High School	Witness and Service	Learn how to share Christ, do ministry.
College Age	Vocation and Calling	Determine gifts, interest, and aptitude.

When Kids Challenge Church Attendance

"My twelve-year-old says church is boring. I don't want to turn him off to church by forcing him to attend. Should I let him stay home?" asked a frustrated mom. "Just three months ago, he loved to go; now he says the Sunday School teacher is boring."

"Kids that age go through lots of changes in every area," I (Tim) told her. "Physically they are growing rapidly, socially experimenting with friendships and roles; mentally beginning to think conceptually, instead of in physical and concrete terms. Sometimes these changes make church difficult, so they challenge your church attendance tradition."

"You mean it's not just Jason?"

"Oh, no! Most kids his age face the same issue. He may feel intimidated socially—most church groups include kids from lots of different schools. Maybe he has to sit next to a developed, taller girl. Perhaps the teacher is using language that doesn't stimulate his new mental capabilities. It may not be that Sunday School is boring, but that he doesn't feel comfortable there. Try not to get sucked into the emotion of his rejecting it; he's not rejecting God. Let him know you go to church as a family. His choice may be to join you in the worship service instead of Sunday School, or help out in one of the preschool classes. Ask him to let you know which he chooses."

"In other words, church attendance is not negotiable?"

"Right, but you are giving him choices, and that may be the real issue. Jason may simply be testing the limits. But deep down inside he knows he needs limits. At this stage it is common to push against them."

"Some parents let their children choose whether or not they'll go to church when they're twelve."

"That's like saying, 'It's not important enough for us to set a limit and enforce it.' The child interprets, *church must not be that important.* Twelve is too young to make a wise decision on something so critical. Kids that age don't understand their own emotions, let alone the issues. But youth groups are like clothes—they have different styles and appeal to different types of teens. When a youth turns sixteen, he can drive himself to another youth group. Allow him to choose one that teaches the Bible, has reliable and trained leadership, and that makes you feel comfortable.

> .....
>
> ### Family Night
>
> Every Friday we aim for Family Night. We eat something for dinner that everyone likes. Dad does the devotion and we pray, kneeling at the couch. We then play indoor hide-and-peek and/or another family game. We pop lots of popcorn and watch a wholesome video movie with the kids.
>
> *Dawn Van Drunen, Colorado Springs, CO*
>
> .....

"You maintain the value that you want your teen involved, but you are training him to take responsibility for his own spiritual nurture. Another variation is to say, 'We go together on Sundays, but if you want to go to another youth group or parachurch group on the weekdays you can do that.' I have seen many teens get more out of Campus Life or Young Life than their church youth group. But remember, you have more influence on their spiritual growth at home than the teacher does with a forty-five minute class once a week. Put your emphasis there."

Parents influence their children's spiritual development. We don't resign our jobs as spiritual nurturers just because kids challenge us. We teach spiritual life skills to our children: how to worship, how to pray, how to study the Bible, how to serve others, and the importance of being in a small group for accountability and care. But one of the most powerful influencers will be our example. Dave Veerman says,

When I look back on my life, I realize that one of the reasons I have been so heavily involved in local churches throughout my life is the example my parents set. Both were very involved in church, singing in the choir, counseling at camp, serving on a variety of boards and committees, having the pastors and missionaries over for dinner, and participating in small-group Bible studies. I learned from watching my parents that an important expression of my faith in Christ is involvement with a local body of believers. Model the right values to your children.[4]

Stay Close

When your preteens challenge your hallowed family traditions, you may feel betrayed, but this is a time when they need you to pull closer. In fact, it may be a test to see if you love them unconditionally. "I will always love you" means you love them even when they are challenging the way you've always done things.

In over twenty years of youth ministry I (Tim) have discovered that teens who challenge a rule, or me as an authority figure, are usually the ones who need attention. In some cases, it is their way of asking for help or making a request for relationship. We want to spend more time with a youth that is acting out and crossing the rules. In their effort to push us away, we reach out and pull them in. To reduce the possibility of children rebelling, stay close. Researchers Merton and Irene Strommen found that teens who had affectionate and caring parents resisted negative behaviors better, and were freer to develop as individuals than their peers:

There is significantly less social alienation among adolescents whose parents emphasize nurturance, as well as less involvement in drug or alcohol use and sexual activity. In nurturing homes we find more adolescents who know how to make

*friends and maintain good relationships with them; more who
are involved in helping-type behaviors and more who tend to
view religion as a liberating and challenging force in their
lives.*[5]

Gail and I (Otis) were watching the wife of a nationally
famous evangelist interviewed on TV when the host asked a
loaded question.

"Your son left the faith for a while, didn't he? Didn't that
hurt you? Weren't you angry with him? He didn't hold to your
traditions."

"What you say is true, but I was not angry."

Before she could continue her statement, the host broke in
and asked another question, seemingly designed to elicit an
emotional reply.

"Now that he is back in the fold, would you have handled
him differently if you had it to do over again?"

"Yes," she smiled. "I would have loved him more."

This response brought gooseflesh to my arms. It was unexpected. More often than not, a parent's response is alienation or
retaliation. Shunning instead of embracing. Moving away when
we should be drawing closer. A teen told me recently that his
rejection of family tradition was a response to a feeling of
unworthiness: "My parents think our family is almost perfect.
To tell them a teacher asked for sexual favors would mean I
would be responsible for shattering it." He was saying, even
though nothing of a physical nature occurred, he did not believe
he merited being a family member. He figured the information
would devastate his family unit. The easier thing to do was to
break away. But his parents were savvy. They intensified the
relationship. Later, when all was settled between his family and
the school, he admitted pulling away was actually a plea for
help.

Keep Learning _____

A mark of a growing person is an openness to learning new things. As children mature through developmental stages, it provides parents opportunities to grow with them. Each stage brings new changes and challenges to everyone. A wise parent embraces each stage and seeks to learn all he can from it. If we are growing along with our child, we are more likely to develop traditions that are flexible and meaningful. Remember, the form of the tradition is dynamic, the value that we seek to pass on is *constant*.

How do we know if we are learning? We need to have some form of measurement. If your child is in school, she receives a report card to measure her progress in learning. Why don't we have report cards for parents? Good idea, isn't it?

The Parent Report Card

Parent's name _____   Date _____

Child's name _____

Evaluation period _____ to _____

Circle the grade for each of the following that your parent has earned:

1. Spends time with me	A B C D F
2. Listens to me	A B C D F
3. Helps me with my homework if I need it	A B C D F
4. Makes the rules clear	A B C D F
5. Is consistent in enforcing the rules	A B C D F
6. Doesn't yell at me when angry	A B C D F
7. Treats all the kids in the family fairly	A B C D F
8. Keeps fun in our family	A B C D F
9. Shows me a good example by completing chores	A B C D F
10. Tries to make holidays special	A B C D F
11. Is building family traditions	A B C D F
12. Shows and tells me he/she loves me	A B C D F
13. Shows respect to me and my friends	A B C D F
14. Lets me make my own decisions	A B C D F
15. Lets me act my age	A B C D F
16. Citizenship (attitude)	A B C D F

Comments:

You may want to make copies of the Parent Report Card and provide them to your children for regular evaluations. Then again, you probably don't! But seriously, when our children see that we are trying to grow along with them, it reduces the rebellion potential. It gives them a chance to have a say, be understood, and know their opinion is valued. You might want to provide these reports once a year or once a month—it's up to you.

A family in Colorado used a variation of the Parent Report Card with their children once a month. They showed me (Tim) their most recent report card; it wasn't all As and Bs. Their children, ages eight, ten, and fifteen, had been trained to be honest and to think critically. They were courageous to record less than favorable grades and comments on their parents' report cards. The father said, "I need to work on some areas. I know what they are. Without the report card, I would falsely assume I was doing a good job, but I wasn't. Why shouldn't we have accountability and feedback at home?"

"Do they like doing this?" I asked.

His fifteen-year-old son interrupted: "Don't let him tell you we like it. I think it stinks!"

Instead of giving him the evil eye, the father smiled at Derek, recognizing his sense of humor.

"My dad is all into this family togetherness thing," Derek continued. "He dreams up stuff like this to keep us all talking and feeling good about each other. He always tells people we like to do this, but it's a hassle."

"Would you like it better if you didn't have these report cards?"

After a short pause, Derek smiled at his father, "Nah, if I want, I can really rip on the old man." Derek's smile grew as he reached out to side-hug his dad.

Derek, a normal, sarcastic teenage boy, had an affectionate

connection with his father that was rare. I wanted to know more about their family. As it turns out, they had weekly family nights, monthly family traditions, monthly parent report cards, a host of holiday traditions—and a teenager!

You see—it *is* possible!

→ Chapter 10 ←

Traditions
of Dedication

⟨∞⟩⟨∞⟩

*I*n the 1992 Barcelona Olympics, a young man named Derek Redmond had earned a position on the British track team as a four-hundred-meter runner. Years before he had dedicated himself to the task, begun to train, and worked his way through the Olympic trials. Thousands of hours of grueling workouts, appetite in submission to a regimented diet, and shaping his mind for the mental stress, had now boiled down to one purpose: win the race.

Hoopla aside, the serious business of competing for the prize began. In the semifinals, his heat rounded three corners and were coming out of the last one. The prize was in sight. With a grimace ambushing his face, Derek grasped for the back of his left leg.

The unthinkable happened.

Derek began to hop, dragging a hurt leg. His upright position soon gave way to bending and almost collapsing to the track. He had pulled a hamstring.

Then a shadow appeared on the track. It began moving toward and around him. When the camera angle changed, it revealed a man running onto the track. He grabbed Derek's left arm and placed it around his neck, helping him to the finish line.

"You can't do that," an official shouted.

"You bet I can," came the retort. "I'm his dad."

Leaning on his father's shoulder, Derek finished the race.

PRINCIPLE : Finishing a commitment is more important than starting.

INTENTIONAL IMPACT: I will work to impress on my children the delight of beginning a process, and the satisfaction of fulfilling it.

Derek had dedicated his life to this race—and not just to stand on the starting line. He did it with the intention to finish. He accomplished his goal with a little help from his dad. It is essential to keep that thought in mind when dedicating yourself or anyone else to a calling or purpose.

Dedication is without question a noble act. The intention is to help insure the person or thing being dedicated has an auspicious beginning. We want things to bode well for the future. But, as in Derek's case, dedication has more to do with *finishing* than beginning.

Beginning costs, but finishing pays.

C.S. Lewis says,

> · · · · ·
> ## Wedding Journal
> After our daughter's wedding, we gave her and her new husband two blank books in which I had copied all the prayers I had written in journals since she was conceived. The two volumes were titled, "Prayers from a Mama's Heart." Her husband loved it as much as she did, because he read her whole life's story. They were both motivated to be prayer partners for their children.
> *Sandy Owsley, San Jose, CA*
> · · · · ·

But we are tethered to Hope that will promise anything without blushing . . . therefore neither ashore nor in the hollow ships will any praise be given to an act on which the doer does not stake his life.[1]

Deepen the Spiritual Roots of Family _____

PRINCIPLE : Dedication traditions can deepen the spiritual roots of family.

INTENTIONAL IMPACT: Because our family belongs to God. I will create opportunities to intentionally impress upon my children the value of a life dedicated to the principles found in Scripture.

Dedication Ceremonies for Children

One of the most important and memorable days of your life has finally arrived! Your tribe has increased. A child is born and you begin to feel the remarkable responsibility balancing on your shoulders. Slowly it dawns on you that you must look somewhere for some help. You've got to take this child over life's bumps and chuckholes, through the tears and laughter, running, walking, or sometimes just toughing out the daily grind. No one else can do it. Only you can be Mommy or Daddy to this little life. You remember the couple in your neighborhood who took their baby to church and dedicated him. A light goes on!

There are two primary ceremonies for setting apart children: infant baptism and dedication, depending on your church tradition. The ceremony outlined here can be used for either.

Choosing to dedicate a baby is a serious decision and cannot be taken lightly. It is NOT to be confused with salvation. Dedication of a baby is lifelong parental commitment to be available to your child for spiritual guidance and to intentionally lead her to the knowledge of God in Jesus Christ. Profound consideration should be given to this tradition. Questions that

demand an answer before the ceremony are:
- Am I willing to make this lifelong commitment?
- Am I willing to model scriptural moral values in word and deed?
- Am I willing to be faithful in church attendance and giving, so that these are illustrated for my child? (We hope this doesn't sound preachy; we feel strongly about this.)

Although parents are powerless to determine the eternal future of their child, they must be aware of the responsibility to be an example and point the way. Upon the dedication of a baby, they are declaring that they will make every effort to create an environment in which the spiritual life of their child can prosper, and their child will be instructed in the basics of the faith. This is more *parent* dedication than *baby* dedication.

Like any ceremony, baby/parent dedication requires thought and planning. First, decide when it will be: a few days, a few weeks, or perhaps even months after birth? (If you have a colicky baby, you may want to wait a couple of months so that everyone will be more comfortable during the ceremony.) You will need to focus on what is being said, and the questions that are being asked. Call the pastor who will officiate the ceremony to help you choose a date. Inform grandparents, aunts and uncles, and special friends. If grandparents or other family members cannot be present at the dedication ceremony, ask someone to stand in their place who has been a mentor, or a friend who has been influential in the life of your family. Choose carefully, because the ones who stand with you will hold you accountable for the parental vows you will be taking.

The dedication ceremony usually takes place during a church service. The pastor will call for the parents and attendants to bring the child to be dedicated. Appropriate questions are directed to the parents regarding the commitment they are making for the future of their child. The pastor then will offer a prayer of dedication. This is a moving and thoughtful time for the entire congregation. It can cause the audience to reflect on their own responsibility as parents. It's a time of renewal and encouragement, a "spiritual checkup" to see their commitment as ongoing.

If your church gives certificates at the ceremony, call the church office ahead of time with the birth information. Certificates vary, but most call for full name of the baby, birth date, date of dedication, and names of mother and father. The minister usually signs the certificate. A video recording is a great way to share this moment with your child when he is older (if the church allows recording in a service). You may want to plan a celebration dinner for family and a few friends after the service.

> .....
>
> *Christmas Game*
>
> We created a "Christmas Memories" game that spurs memories in areas such as foods, Christmas cards and letters, music, snow, decorations, trees, past gifts for Jesus, and preparing (this year) for Jesus.
>
> *Lori Davis, Wheaton, IL.*
>
> ....

As your child grows and matures, talk often of the day when God gave him to you, and of the day you gave him back to God. Talk about who attended and what was said. Perhaps you will want to watch a video of the ceremony together on an anniversary of the promise. Let your child know the significance of the dedication vow. And most importantly, let your son or daughter see God in you.

Becoming a Member of God's Forever Family

When my (Otis) children began to ask questions about receiving Jesus, Gail and I were overcome with mixed feelings. Oh, we wanted more than anything for them to be Christians, but we wanted to be careful that they weren't coerced by our excitement. Children will do things because they want to please.

This can be especially true if they feel they are on the bad side of Mom or Dad. Care in this area cannot be overstated. The following guidelines will be useful to parents in that situation. They are taken from Gail's child growth and development notes. Familiarize yourself with them to feel comfortable in your role as spiritual leader in the home.

*How to Lead Your Child to Christ*____

Some things to consider ahead of time:
- Realize that God is more concerned about your child's eternal destiny and happiness than you are. "The Lord is not slack concerning his promise, ... but is longsuffering to us-ward, not willing that any should perish, but that all should come to repentance" (2 Peter 3:9 KJV).
- Beforehand, pray specifically that God will give you insights and wisdom in dealing with each child on his maturity level.
- Don't use terms like "take Jesus into your heart," "dying and going to hell," or "accepting Christ as your personal Savior." Children are either too literal ("How does Jesus breathe in my heart?"), or the words are too cliché and trite for their understanding.
- Deal with each child alone and don't be in a hurry. Make sure she understands; discuss it until she does. Take your time.

A few cautions:
- When drawing children to Himself, Jesus said ALLOW them to come to Him. Only with adults did He use the term COMPEL. Do not *compel* children. See Mark 10:14, and Luke 14:23.
- Remember that unless God Himself is speaking through the Holy Spirit to the child, there will be no genuine heart experience of regeneration. Parents, don't get caught up in the idea

that Jesus will return the day *before* you were going to speak to your child about salvation, and that it will be too late. Look at God's character—He *IS* love! He is not dangling your child's soul over hell. Wait on God's timing. Pray, with faith, believing. Be concerned, but don't push.

The plan:
Prepare ahead of time and know the Scriptures to use.

• *God loves you.* Recite John 3:16. Recite it again with your child's name in place of "the world."

• *You need the Savior.* Deal with sin carefully. Say, "there is one thing that cannot enter heaven—SIN." Be sure the child knows what sin is. Ask her to name some. (Things common to children—lying, sassing, disobeying, etc.). Sin is DOING or THINKING anything wrong according to God's Word.

• *Ask, "Have you sinned?"* If the answer is, "No," do NOT continue. Assure him that when he does feel like he has sinned, to come and talk to you again. Some parents may want to have prayer, thanking God "for this young child who is willing to do what is right." Make it easy for him to talk to you again, but do not continue. Do not say, "Oh, yes, you have too sinned!" and then name some. With children, wait for God's conviction.

If the answer is "Yes," continue. He may even give a personal illustration of some sin he has done recently or one that has bothered him.

• Tell him what God says about sin: *We've all sinned.* "There is none righteous, no, not one" (Rom. 3:10 KJV). "For all have sinned, and come short of the glory of God" (Rom. 3:23 KJV). **Because of that sin, we can't get to God,** "For the wages of sin is death . . . " (Rom. 6:23 KJV); **so He had to come to us,** ". . . but the gift of God is eternal life through Jesus Christ our Lord" (Rom. 6:23 KJV).

• *Relate God's gift of salvation to receiving Christmas gifts—we* don't earn this gift or pay for it; we just accept it and are thankful for it.

• *Make a definite decision.* Explain that Christ must be received if salvation is to be possessed, but remember, DO NOT FORCE A DECISION. Ask your child to pray, out loud, in his own words. Give him some things he could say if he seems unsure. It is best to avoid having the child repeat a prayer after you; let him think and make it personal. If you wish to guide your child though prayer, here is suggested language:

> *Dear God, I know that I am a sinner [have child name specific sins he or she acknowledged earlier, such as lying, stealing, disobeying, etc.]. I know that Jesus died on the cross to pay for all my sins. I ask you to forgive me of my sins. I believe that Jesus died for me and rose from the dead, and I now take Him as my Savior. Thank You for loving me. In Jesus' name. Amen."*

Now be prepared for a blessing! After salvation has occurred, you pray for him out loud. Pronounce a blessing on your child.

• *God will never leave you.* Show her that she will be able to keep her relationship open with God through repentance and forgiveness (just like with her family and friends), and that God will always love her. "I will never leave thee, nor forsake thee" (Heb. 13:5 KJV).

• *Teach him his "family" responsibilities*—The Big Five. Show now that he is a member of God's family, His child, he has some responsibilities: (1) to pray, (2) to know more about God (reading the Bible), (3) to love God's church, (4) to love others (The Golden Rule: "Do unto others as you would have them do unto you"), and (5) to give to God's work.

When your child makes this beautiful step of faith, you will, of course, want to mark it on your calendar and on your time line. It is the most significant decision anyone will ever make. The occasion is a watershed in life. Future determinations will be affected by this choice. Some families celebrate it as a birthday until the child turns a predetermined age, because children sometimes forget how important this decision is and begin to doubt their commitment (especially when struggling with bad behavior). The yearly celebration serves to reinforce the dedication of their life to God. Don't forget to write the date on your time line in Chapter 11.

Baptism

"See that soldier walking across the street, Danny," Charles said to his nine year old. "Well, that uniform he is wearing is kind of like baptism. It doesn't make him a soldier. It only identifies him as one. Baptism is the suit we wear. It doesn't make us a Christian. It only identifies us as one" (1 Peter 3:21).

About a year before, Danny had prayed to become a member of God's family. He was asking to be baptized. "Why can't I? All my friends have been."

Danny is at a milestone in his life and Charles wants to make the best of it. But he is right to be cautious. Baptism isn't a fad. It isn't a club. It is a step of obedience to God, and children need to understand its significance. Charles wants his son to grasp its meaning and know what kind of commitment he is making as he goes into the water.

> .....
>
> ## Table Grace
>
> At the dinner table, we sometimes offer a prayer with a response. When my son began to offer prayers, he nearly always ended with, "And today we praise your name." This became a refrain that the entire family can repeat after thanks is offered for the food. Every so often we vary the refrain, but using a refrain encourages everyone to participate in the prayer rather than just waiting for someone to say it so the eating can begin.
>
> *Susan Miller, Colorado Springs, CO*
>
> ....

One of the most significant spiritual events we can celebrate is our child's baptism, publicly declaring faith in Christ, death to self, and willingness to live a new life under Christ's lord-ship. Baptism is also a connection to the past. It not only signi-fies the death, burial, and resurrection of our Lord, it identifies us with a long line of people—our spiritual ancestors all the way back to Abraham. The male children of Abraham were identified as connected to him by the rite of circumcision. That was a distinguishing mark that set his offspring apart from other families. That rite is no longer required for identification with God (Gal. 6:15). A new badge is worn by today's believers. It is baptism. It is an identifying factor of circumcision of heart.

To prepare your child and yourself for the baptismal service, you might springboard from the following.

1. Discuss baptism on a family night. You may have every-one dress in clothes to represent different cultures or occupa-tions. Talk about who everyone looks like. Do the clothes make them who they are?

2. Take your family to a baptismal service. Afterward, encourage everyone to talk about it and share their observa-tions.

3. During the week, get permission from the church to visit the baptismal dressing rooms. Walk to the baptismal pool to get her familiar with the location.

4. Plan the day of the ceremony. How will you celebrate?

5. Have the camera ready to record this historic tradition.

6. Together with your child, mark it on the time line.

Roman Sanchez, a pastor to middle school students, initiated a family celebration, inviting the parents of those being baptized to join him for a pizza party afterward. Following the simple lunch, he presents a personal word of affirmation for each stu-dent along with a certificate of baptism and small gift (usually a Christian book). It is powerful for parents, and family members who aren't believers, to witness affirmation of the spiritual growth of the child.

When our (Tim) daughters were baptized, each wore a formal purple velvet dress to signify royalty, because they were now members of God's family—princesses, as daughters of the King. We created formal invitations for family and close friends to come to the special event at church and Sunday dinner, featuring a favorite cake saying, "Congratulations on Your Baptism." Brooke's had a blue river running through the middle. Nicole's cake had frogs on it—not for any spiritual reason, but because she loves frogs! Video cameras rolled, still cameras flashed, joyous tears streamed. We presented an engraved leather Bible, inscribed as to the significance of our daughter's decision and how pleased we were to see her take this important step, and a gold cross necklace with a note encouraging, "always stand up for Jesus." Some of the guests offered Christian music or books, clothes, or fancy hair clips.

First Communion

Another monument along the path of spiritual growth is the Lord's Supper. The service itself has various ways of being observed, but all Christians and churches agree to its significance. Jesus Himself gave the instructions, "This do in remembrance of me" (Luke 22:19 KJV). Jesus paved the way with that statement for us to be connected to Him until He comes, an awesome reminder of the tradition within this act of service.

Each time their church observed the Lord's Table, Mr. and Mrs. Hall made sure their children sat between them. As the service progressed, they explained each step on a child's level. As each child's first Communion arrived, he was well versed in what he was observing and what participation meant.

When you celebrate a child's first Communion, talk about it on the way home. A journal entry in a daily calendar, daily planner, or a diary will freeze the moment in time. Be sure to mark it on the spiritual time line.

Facing the Teen Years _____

As your children mature, you'll want to be ready for the challenges of the teen years. Remember the intentional impact you're working toward: to create opportunities to intentionally impress upon your children the value of a life dedicated to the principles found in Scripture.

Why should you talk with your children about sex, as well as model a loving relationship at home?

1. It is your responsibility and your privilege.

2. No one knows your child like you do or loves him or her as much as you do.

3. Children learn more about relationships from example than from any other method of learning.

4. Sexuality is best understood in context of a marriage exhibiting affection, patience, sacrifice, understanding, and romance. Single parents can model appropriate affection and care in their male-female relationships.

5. To inform you about their fears and misinformation about love, sex, dating, and to give you a context to correct and protect them.

6. When you are open to talking about a difficult topic, you are demonstrating unconditional love and even when tough, attempting to connect with your child.

7. God has designed the home to be a place of learning about love and sexuality.

8. Conversation about sex is one more way you prepare your children to make wise choices.[2]

A Dating Dedication

When Nicole met a boy she wanted to go out with, we (Tim) discussed with her that she needed to ask permission—not to start dating, but to prepare for it. She did. We said, "You are ready to date when you know the benefits of dating, the dangers of dating, and have a personal commitment to your dating standards, including who you will go out with, physical standards, and other covenants. All of these must be given careful thought and in writing."

"Okay, Dad," she responded cheerfully.

Forty-five minutes later, she came back with three handwritten pages of her Dating Covenant. We discussed it, prayed about her dating life, and then ordered pizza to celebrate her readiness for dating.

The Chastity Challenge
"What?"

When that word is said with an upward swing in tone, it snaps us to attention. It says to the hearer there is wonder in the question. It is doubt and curiosity mixed with demand that a follow-up question clarify the challenge.

The Apostle Paul follows that question with, "Do you not know . . ."

More doubt and curiosity. More room for more clarification.

" . . . your body is a temple of the Holy Spirit, who is in you? . . . You are not your own; you were bought at a price" (1 Cor. 6:19-20 NIV).

These questions make a statement. They are eye-openers to our vulnerability in everyday choices. They are a call to caution. Following are eight reasons to remain a virgin until marriage. Copy this page and encourage your child to keep it on a bulletin board or in a diary.

Eight Reasons
To Remain a Virgin until Marriage

1. To protect you from making the sexual part of life too big a deal. Playing around with sex can become obsessive and addictive. It may begin to control you, developing a depraved mind (Rom. 1), causing grief and pain.

2. To prevent distrust of your spouse in marriage. If you give in to the sex pull now, you will live with the unspoken question: will I be able to control my sex drive when I am married?

3. To protect you from guilt and its accompanying anger and depression. It's awkward to gaze into your spouse's eyes on your wedding night and say, "Honey, I give you myself, but you aren't the first."

4. To prevent low self-esteem. Teens who have premarital sex have a lower view of themselves because they gave in to temptation.

5. To protect against the risk of pregnancy. Unless you are ready to be a parent and take on all the responsibilities, sex is a risky thing to do.

6. To prevent sexually transmitted diseases and protect you against the HIV virus (AIDS). Teenagers who engage in sex are more likely to acquire medical problems. Don't buy the *safe* sex lie! Even using a condom, there is risk of disease.

7. To prevent a seared conscience. If you ignore God's truth here, you are likely to become cold and hard in other areas as well, leading to callousness toward God and His Word.

8. To protect you from sexual confusion and homosexuality. Those who experiment early with sex often have negative experiences that create strong images—repelling a person from having sex with someone of the opposite gender.[3]

Because so many teens admit to sexual activity today, more and more parents are turning to a chastity challenge for their children. It is more than a vow on the part of their children. It is also a vow of support from parents. A support that says, *You may talk to me at any time about anything. There will be no upbraiding, no "I can't believe you said that" lectures, and no "I can't deal with this" attitudes.*

Boys as well as girls are keeping these vows. Purity isn't singular to one gender.

> . . . . .
>
> *Grandchild's Journal*
>
> When our grandchildren were born, we purchased a journal-memory book. We have been recording events about their heritage, with the emphasis on their spiritual heritage. We will present these to them in the future.
>
> Sandy Owsley, San Jose, CA
>
> . . . .

Commemorating the Vow

"One of the most precious things I own, I wear on my finger," says Charity Laughlin. "It is a purity ring given to me by my parents." Her eyes fall to admire the ring. "First, it symbolizes a covenant I made with God. I will save the gift of sexuality He has given me, until I can give it within the bonds of marriage. Second, it represents a principle passed to me by my parents. They enjoyed the benefits of waiting until marriage, and have taught me how important waiting for sex is for my marriage."

"So the ring has meaning for the future?"

"Not just for the future," Charity explains, "It is a daily reminder of my responsibility to me, and whomever I date." She wrinkles her nose and admits, "Mom and Dad can't go with me on dates, but this ring does. It's always with me to prompt me about my promise."

Charity's parents had a diamond set in the middle of her

ring. When she decides to marry, that stone will be taken from her ring and set in the ring she will give her husband. That same diamond will always be a reminder to him of the purity she took to the altar. She says she wears the ring proudly and will explain its meaning to anyone who asks.

To observe the tradition of the Chastity Challenge, whether it's for a son or daughter, you don't have to purchase a ring with a diamond or an expensive watch. A necklace, bracelet, or any piece of jewelry that can represent the vow will function as the point of purity.

When you present the jewelry, make it a special day. Go on a date with your child. Openly talk about sex and its role in marriage. Explain the virtues of remaining chaste. Tell him you are making a vow with him—one of support, and that you will be there for him through the difficulty of maintaining chastity in a relationship. After the vows, stay connected to your child and his relationships. We're not saying hang around and be a pain, but let the strength of your support and love be a blessing.

The Vow to Stay Off Drugs

We are custodians of the temple where the Holy Spirit resides. No deeper invitation to virtue could ever be given than this one. We don't own an exclusive contract to our bodies. When explaining this truth to children, our objective is to furnish them with the information needed to make right choices even when the crowd does not. If our teens understand that their bodies belong to God, the choice to not drink, smoke, or take drugs may become easier.

In the course of a conversation along these lines, my (Otis) older children, Matt and Becky, made a promise to their mother without prompting. They pledged that neither drugs or alcohol would ever enter their bodies. Although the vow was not in the context of any ceremony, it meant a lot to Gail and me. As parents, it was a milestone in our family's progress toward unity. Many families are creating a tradition around this principle. They are observing it close to the age of ten because of the availability of the substances.

The Morris family borrowed videos from the local library on the dangers of substance abuse. They planned a family night. After viewing the tapes, they illustrated what happens when a person is out of control. Of course they didn't get drunk, but simulated it by spinning each other in a chair. Then with a nerf pistol, they tried to hit a target called "purity." No one could hit the target. The lesson was obvious. They discussed the Scripture, "Do not get drunk on wine, which leads to debauchery. Instead, be filled with the Spirit" (Eph. 5:18). After the lesson, each child was asked to consider signing a contract which illustrated deeding their bodies to the Holy Spirit. Mom and Dad asked them to make every decision about substance use by always first consulting the One who lives within.

Communicating on these issues becomes another monument on the spiritual growth chart of each child.

→ Chapter 11 ←

Rite-of-Passage Traditions

*Y*oung adults frequently wonder, *At what point in life do I pass from childhood into adulthood?* Because it remains unanswered, most are resolved to ignore the question at best. Or at worst, they live in the "Peter Pan Syndrome," the reluctance to leave the joys of childhood and enter the responsibilities of adulthood. Many have yet to advance in choices of life because they have never been told it is OK to be and to think like an adult.

When children approach the age of fifteen, the relationship between them and their parents moves to a different style. We call it the "coaching" period. Children no longer require the kind of parenting previously needed. Now they go into the real world to stretch their wings. They begin to test the values learned in their homes against authentic life circumstances. They want to experience things for themselves. Obviously, they are still too young to be left alone in this venture, so parents shift into a different role alongside teens.

Watching from the sidelines, we observe our children gain experience in the game of life. When precepts are not followed or when they stagger under the decision-making process, we call them to the bench and help with instruction, then send them back into the game with our support. This era marks the end of childhood and the transition into adulthood called adolescence. It is here we believe a rite of passage is necessary to answer the question, "When do I pass from childhood to adulthood?"

Letting Go

Parents must begin releasing the rope that has bound their child to them by the time the child is about fifteen. It will mean grasping the last opportunities to make an impression prior to the spreading of the child's wings. Parents who hold too tightly find themselves smarting from the sting of rope burn as the reins are jerked from their hands. Parents may ask, *How can I correctly loosen my grip? With what do I want my child equipped as I prepare to send him out into the world? Where is he going? Can I be sure he will make the right decisions?*

> . . . . .
>
> ### Feeding on the Word
> When we are together for a meal, I like to read a short passage of Scripture and discuss it for a few minutes.
> Mark DeVries, Nashville, TN
>
> . . . .

People brought up in the same family environment often go different directions morally, making opposite choices though taught the same values. The freedom to make choices can never be stolen from an individual. That freedom can only be willingly surrendered by the individual to a more engaging life option. Rite-of-passage traditions can be the measuring stick for a child's spiritual growth. Celebrate them intentionally. They won't happen by accident.

PRINCIPLE : Milestones in the life of a child are important and should be marked with significant ceremony or commemoration.

INTENTIONAL IMPACT: We will establish rites of passage in the life of our children representing freedom of choice coupled with adult accountability.

Our (Otis) daughter Leah's height is measured and marked on the hall doorjamb. It is a visual reminder of her consistent physical growth. Had the marks not moved up over the months, we would have consulted a doctor about why she was not growing. I wonder, if parents decided to measure their child's spiritual growth in a similar manner and the marks didn't move up, would they be as unsettled? Would they seek help from respected spiritual counselors? Many do not.

The growth marks from childhood through adolescence leading to the commencement of spiritual adulthood can be blurred by many things: ignorance of stages in the child's life, not enough time to parent, apathetic parenting, or even simply parenting by accident (what I call crisis parenting). Blurred lines are why we urge parents to become *intentional* about creating milestones in the lives of their children.

> *Personal Notebook*
>
> **Whenever our children think of things they cannot live without, we have them write those items in a personal notebook. They can save their allowance for these items or ask for them for Christmas, birthday, Sister's Day, etc. When a gift-giving event comes along, we have a reminder of the things they would want.**
>
> *Lori Davis, Wheaton, IL*

Growth lines create clear visual markers for a child to remember. Taking into consideration *spiritual, emotional*, and *social* aspects of life, milestones will occur at differing intervals.

There comes a time in every child's life when the interval between adolescence and spiritual adulthood must be bridged. The connection should be remembered by placing a symbolic monument in her life, a mark on her spiritual doorjamb to remind the child that it's OK to become an adult. It serves to prompt her to take responsibility for her own decisions and actions as a spiritual grown-up. What is the best way to accomplish that task? Let us suggest several ways to do it.

The Blessing Retreat

Think about the time that Issac was tricked by his second son, Jacob, into receiving the blessing before the firstborn, Esau. Realizing what happened, Issac explains, " 'I have blessed him, [Jacob] and indeed he shall be blessed.' When Esau heard the words of his father, he cried with an exceeding great and bitter cry, and said to his father, 'Bless me, even me also, O my father!'" (Gen. 27:31-34 NKJV) This is a pained cry from a young man who could not bear the thought of living without his father's blessing. For whatever reason, there are many men and women who have never received a blessing of love, value, and affirmation from their parents. Their cry may not be as loud, nor articulated as well as Esau's, but their dilemma is just as painful.

I (Tim) was attending a Promise Keepers meeting at the Los Angeles Coliseum. At the conclusion, the speaker asked us to stand if we were willing to be better dads. Thousands stood to their feet, including me. As I surveyed the crowd of sixty thousand men, most were standing. I assumed they were fathers. I knew they were passionately committing to do something for which most probably did not have the skills. I knew that inspiration without instruction leads to frustration. I turned to a friend and said, "We don't have a clue how to implement what we are saying we will do."

"You're right," my friend answered.

My perplexity launched me into a study of the Bible and what men need to do to become better dads. I discovered the need to give and receive *The Blessing*. Based on Isaac's blessing of his sons in Genesis 27, I decided to plan a weekend retreat targeted at boys ten to twenty years old. Wanting to build a rite-of-passage event, memorable to both father and son, we instructed them on the five points of a biblical blessing, spelling out BLESS:

Bond physically—express appropriate affection.
Lifelong friendship—invest in strengthening the relationship.
Esteem highly—express love and respect for each other.
Spoken word—affirm your son's character and personhood.
Special future—create vision by expressing faith and hope.

The fathers took their sons for a hike, presenting these five points through hugs, commitments of time, affirming words, presentations of gifts, and a written covenant of blessing. The hike became a monument. When they returned, the sons stood in an inner circle surrounded by their dads, who placed their right hands on their shoulders and their left hands on the shoulder of the man beside them.

"This circle represents the brotherhood of Christ," I explained. "We welcome each son here. We don't see you as a boy, we see you as a brother in Christ. Welcome! You are no longer a boy, but you are a son. You are a son of God. You are no longer a boy, but a man. Leave childish things and pursue maturity in Christ."

Some of the sons began to get misty eyes.

"Look around the circle," I continued. "These men are your brothers in Christ, they are here to support you. They are here to support your fathers. But they are also here to hold each other accountable. As brothers, we are to 'speak the truth in love' as 'iron sharpens iron.' We really do need each other."

I asked the fathers to affirm their sons in the company of men. Each dad verbally affirmed his son in front of the others. It was a powerful experience. Then I asked the sons to express appreciation to their fathers. Tears began to roll.

Ethan began to sob. "I don't spend that much time with my dad," he said. "He works a lot. I wasn't sure my dad loved me, but after this weekend, I know he does. I am so proud of my dad, and proud to be his son."

As he said this, his father broke down in tears. He told me later he had never heard those words, "I am proud of my dad and proud to be his son."

We also designed father/daughter and mother/daughter retreats along with parent/child Heritage Builder events. These include single-parent families as well as two-parent families.

> *Menorah Noel*
> We celebrate Hanukkah (I'm a Jewish believer) by lighting the menorah eight days in a row. We hide a present for our daughter. The focus is on the gift. On Christmas day, we give only a few gifts as we celebrate Jesus' birth, play Christmas music, and have a birthday party for Jesus with a cake, singing "Happy Birthday to Jesus."
> *David Olshine, Columbia, SC*

The Christian Bar Mitzvah

The Bar/Bat Mitzvah is an event positioned on the time line of a child's life, at the beginning of adolescence. (*Bar* is for boys and *Bat* is for girls.) It will become a monument in the path of his past and a guidepost to his future. For the Jewish family it means the child, at the age of thirteen, is deemed ready for religious responsibility. He or she becomes a "Son/Daughter of the Covenant."

For the Christian youth, it is a time when a child assumes responsibility for spiritual disciplines like quiet time in prayer and God's Word. He is responsible for building relationships that glorify God. She seeks to meet and grow with other Christians in Bible studies, Christian retreats, and uplifting activities that will fuel passion for God. He begins to understand the transition that is taking place in his life as Scripture characterizes: "When I was a child, I talked like a child, I thought like a child, I reasoned like a child. When I became a man, I put childish ways behind me" (1 Cor 13:11).

The Christian Bar/Bat Mitzvah means putting away childish things and accepting the responsibility of adult spiritual disciplines. It is designed to make a significant impact on parent and child.

The following process and ceremony are for families who are already involved with the spiritual growth of their child and want to take a step further. Many churches are picking up this tradition. If you feel inclined to plan a Bar/Bat Mitzvah, simplify and personalize these guidelines to create a tradition that works in the context of your family or church. Use the plan here to inspire and motivate you.

Define the journey

The length of a child's journey to reach the point of responsibility will be determined by the depth of the spiritual basis developed in her home. If possible, begin a year before the actual date of the Bar/Bat Mitzvah to assemble the people and plan the schedule. The timing should reflect the spiritual, emotional, and social growth of the child. It is a good idea to plan the ceremony around a significant birthday. Involve your son or daughter in the planning. All this builds excitement and receptivity to the message of the ceremony. The importance of this event far outweighs the minor problems that may arise in planning it.

If that basis has not been laid for spiritual responsibility, or if the time is not right for the child to establish an adult relationship to God, then a time frame can be created to prepare material and develop maturity. The parent overseeing the process must establish discussions between himself or herself and the child, then begin to move those conversations into topics which will be talked about at the Bar/Bat Mitzvah during the wisdom sharing sessions. Those topics will include the following:

- A man/woman and his/her God
- A man/woman and his/her family
- A man/woman and his/her friends
- A man/woman and his/her job
- A man/woman and his/her spouse
- A man/woman in the world, but not of the world

Pick the wisdom council

One of the best elements of a Christian Bar/Bat Mitzvah is when the youth selects six men/women to sit on the wisdom council. These adults should include one grandparent (if possible) and five other spiritual adults who have influenced his life: a youth director, Sunday School or Christian high school teacher, friend of the family, aunt, uncle, or pastor. The wisdom council will be instructed to foster a continuing relationship with the child, even long distance, if necessary. They will be asked to keep notes of the wisdom they share, participate in wisdom sharing sessions just prior to the ceremony, speak five minutes during the ceremony, and place their notes in a Bible to be given to the youth.

One of the persons selected will be chosen to act as facilitator, guiding the discussions and keeping any one person (including Dad or Mom) from dominating the ceremony. Each of them will introduce one of the six disciplines listed above and tell why it is important. The facilitator will make sure the youth is involved in the discussions.

Plan the event

While managing all the details of the process, there are four ingredients that need to be applied. Together, they give meaning and direction to the overall purpose of the ceremony.

Affirm: The child will sense love from his parents by their participation and involvement. The ceremony serves as a confirmation of a child's salvation and personal relationship with God. The time and fact of the new birth will be visited often throughout the process. Perhaps the wisdom council will give testimony to their own salvation experience.

Inform: The child will receive a wealth of information on what the future holds in the area of her relationship to God, family, employer, friends, spouse, and the world. She will get perspectives from different viewpoints as each selected adult responds in the wisdom sharing sessions one week prior to the event. She will gain a foundational understanding of the meaning of each spiritual discipline.

. . . . .

Brother's Day and Sister's Day

Since we have Mother's Day and Father's Day, we decided to invent Brother's Day and Sister's Day for our kids. We celebrate these on the Sundays between Mother's Day and Father's Day. On their special day, they get to plan the menu, which I type up the night before. So what if we have shrimp, green pepper, pepperoni, sausage, bacon, and waffles all on the same day? Then we try to go on an outing the child wants. We plan these on Sundays so that there will be free time available to do things as a family. We also give them a few gifts.

Lori Davis, Wheaton, IL

. . . .

Evaluate: The sessions will explore the depth of the child's spiritual development, and identify where growth is needed. Weaknesses can be evaluated and addressed. The parent will understand where his child is heading, and which disciplines need attention. A bond is established with the council so that ongoing wisdom may be shared.

Celebrate: The entire process is a celebration of life's transitions, maturation, and growth. It is an applauding of a family's success in bringing up a child in the way he should go (Prov. 22:6). So let the celebration begin and last for a lifetime!

Prior to the ceremony, leave enough time for the wisdom sharing sessions to take place. Then share a catered or a potluck dinner. For the ceremony, the platform or room is set with seven chairs in a semi-circle (six adults plus son or daughter). The wisdom council comes to the platform as they are introduced. It is explained why each was chosen. Each takes about five minutes to:

1. Relate a story about the child and parents. (Humorous is better!)

2. Share the topic he has been given to discuss—and its importance.

3. Lay hands on the child and lead in prayer toward a particular discipline.

4. Give a gift to remember the occasion (gold cross, framed poem, book).

Roles and responsibilities that follow

A new relationship between parent and child is formed through this rite of passage. After the ceremony, the youth should immediately be given responsibility in several areas: choosing relationships, initiating his own quiet times, helping to teach family nights or lead them when Dad or Mom is out of town. These areas will become more defined as time passes, but parents now measure the choices of the young adult by guidelines established by the wisdom council.

When done properly, the weight of the responsibility upon

the child begins to propel her into the right decision-making process. The results of this milestone should be seen in the following areas.

1. It establishes the importance and practice of spiritual discipline in the child's life.

2. It establishes adult accountability relationships.

3. It establishes a new level of communication with the child.

4. It establishes an opportunity for the wisdom council to connect with the girl or boy. The connection may include cards or phone calls on special days.

5. The wisdom council offers ongoing counsel to the parents.

Welcome Your Child to Puberty _____

Puberty! Even the word sounds funny. Be sure there is no one in the room first, then say it out loud by itself. "PUBERTY!" What pictures do those vowels and consonants conjure up in your mind? You have been there, and you know "it ain't no cause to celebrate." A farmer doesn't celebrate when his crop just begins to sprout. And since when do we celebrate confusion, perplexity, or being baffled? Since when are blackheads, whiteheads (and we're not talking hair color here), big feet and skinny legs, smelly armpits, braces, fumble fingers, or squeaky voices things of beauty? If anything, this is a time to forget! *Just ignore me until I can grow a full crop of whatever and get this physique organized*, a kid might say. His nose, feet, teeth, ears, arms, and legs are too big for what he's got. He looks like he was put together by a church committee.

If somehow you have forgotten exactly what puberty feels like, let us suggest a way to jog your memory. When you get up in the morning, put on a suit that's ten sizes too big, then ride your bike down to the financial district and try to do business. How seriously will you be taken? How seriously will you feel about yourself?

. . . . .

The Family Crest

On the fireplace mantle in the Taylor family room is a piece of artwork that has significant meaning. It is their family crest. Its colors, figures, and design have been chosen to represent what the Taylor family is about: an old fashioned scroll "T" with figures between the beautiful flowing lines, purple for the royalty and honor of God, gold for the purity and honesty of relationships, white for the value of truth. A silver cord that wraps around the "T" to represent the silver cord Solomon speaks of in Ecclesiastes 12:6.

The family crest illustrates the tie from past to future. All the children understand the meaning of it and can recite it to anyone who wishes to know. A family crest is a perfect way to picture the values your family holds dear, so the children can become aware of them. It is another noble way to keep your values in front of your children without an "in your face" confrontation, or another "oh, boy, here we go again" lecture.

Perhaps you come from a family that has passed a crest from generation to generation. Great! Keep it going. Make sure your children know what values it represents. If your family has no crest, then you may want to design one. Call the family together and survey each member to find out what values each wants to represent. Choose the colors and what they will symbolize, where the figures will be placed and what they will signify. Refer to it often, reciting how it represents the home.

. . . . .

Well, whatever it is, puberty is a milestone in our lives. Fun to look back on, but not forward to. So, since it happens anyway, why not celebrate? For girls, it's a time they experience their first menstrual period and buy their first bra. I (Otis) remember celebrating those times with my daughters on dates to a local restaurant. I told them I was proud they were becoming ladies. You might want to write a letter of how you love and support them while they are going through all the emotions that accompany growing up.

When my son began to wrestle with growing up, his voice would crack at the most inopportune times. He noticed girls were taller, and that worried him. His coordination was leaving, and he felt like a willowy sapling. Matthew and I had lots of talks. We celebrated by walking down to the local fast-food place to drink a Coke and talk about growing up. We marked it on a calendar. Even now we reminisce about those times.

Preparing for adolescence

Adolescence is a hallway between childhood and adulthood. The problem is that it has a lot of false escape exits. Behind the exit doors are all kinds of things that distract our kids from growing up. Among those are the likes of drugs, alcohol, cultural fads, and the cry of "no boundaries."

We (Otis) had what the Ledbetter family now calls "The Sex Talk." Gail and I figured that kids were going to get information from somewhere, so why not from us? Like other parents, we set a day, time, and place where that talk could occur. As the day drew close, there was an air of anticipation. Hugging, giggling, and snuggling awaited. The kids knew we would go somewhere special. (Some parents take an entire weekend away from the house.)

We took along Dr. Dobson's tape series, *Preparing For Adolescence*, listened, and talked about the wonder of God's beautiful plan. With our daughters, Gail drove to a park, walked and picked leaves, had lunch at a restaurant, drew lots of diagrams on napkins, and answered every question until they couldn't think of any more. Later, they brought the leaves home and dried them. The girls still have them as reminders of the day they joined those "in the know."

The Jones family always commemorated this occasion by planting a tree together in the backyard after "the talk." The date was etched in the bark to remind them of that special day. The tree became a monument and the center of many more conversations through the years during backyard barbecues. Jeff , now grown, tells of times when he goes back to his mom and dad's backyard, and under his tree, remembers what his responsibility is to his own children.

Preparing an atmosphere to talk

Kids get nervous about puberty. The goal is to help children navigate its perils, including their blossoming sexuality. They have heard all kinds of horror stories. Suzanne and I (Tim) have discovered nine tips (which spell out SEXUALITY) to establish the proper atmosphere for a meaningful discussion about it with our children.

1. **S**tart early—Preteens show an interest in their changing bodies. Be open to discuss age-appropriate topics before puberty begins.

2. **E**nvironment—Display affection appropriately in your home. Do you feel safe discussing sensitive topics? How can you nurture that safety?

3. **EX**ample—(I know it doesn't begin with an X, but it's close.) As husbands and wives, we should provide a model of pure and balanced sexuality to our teens. Are you aware of the biblical standards for sexuality? Do you practice them?

4. **U**nderstanding—Be aware of the words and concepts your child will understand as you engage them in conversation. What is accurate and age appropriate?

5. **A**cceptance—We must accept our children as sexual beings. That means we are comfortable with their gender and relaxed when we are alone together with an opposite-sex child.

6. **L**oosen up—Be relaxed, casual, and conversational. Don't lecture. Try to "go with the flow." Don't force the conversation.

7. **I**nitiative—Make the first move. Show that you are open to talk about these issues.

8. **T**ime—Take your time to be gradual and natural. Be willing to be repetitive (that is how children learn). Be willing to use "creative redundancy."

9. **Y**ield—Yield to another time if you sense resistance or a loss of interest. By leaving the conversation open-ended, it is easier to start it next time.[1]

Sixteen—Rights, Roles, Responsibilities _____

Sixteen is considered a milestone by some. Parties are given, and, in some families, that age determines the right to date. But age does not necessarily determine rights at this juncture. Rights, for dating or other privileges or activities, are directly affected by the ability to accept responsibility and the aptitude to slip into the role required by any particular right. If age sixteen did determine the right to date, then the question is, can the teen exhibit proper responsible behavior? Can he show the level of safety required? All these questions, and more like them, need to be answered before rights are randomly handed out.

A savvy parent can take advantage of this age in her teen's life to raise the level of trust required with the new freedom. Freedoms may include driving, music selection, media events, and job opportunities. A meeting with your child may provide opportunity to discuss responsibilities and roles that accompany rights.

The Great Commissioning— High School Graduation _____

PRINCIPLE: It is important to be intentional about blessing our children's future.

INTENTIONAL IMPACT: I will model adult spiritual disciplines to our children so they will duplicate them in future generations.

Certainly one of the great milestones of any teen's days is the commencement of life after high school. With it come mixed emotions that run the gamut from fear of the unknown to the ecstasy of possibility. This is a point of no return. There is no *rewind*, only *fast forward*. What a great place to build a memorial.

The Saturday after graduation, friends of the Golden family were invited to witness a commissioning of the graduate. Mikel's parents had gifts for him, among which were helpful books for college life and a computer he thought he would never get. Mikel's mom displayed photographs that featured friends posed with her son.

Mom and Dad told Mikel they had placed him, early in his life, on a *path* that will lead to a *road* that will turn into a *journey* whose destination is his inner *character*. Friends of his parents spoke of their own graduation and told how they faced their journeys. Mixed in was a little wisdom that would go a long way in helping Mikel watch for potholes along his path. Each of his friends spoke of friendship and pointed out how his positive qualities had influenced them. Before a good meal was served, everyone gathered around Mikel, prayed for his future, and commissioned him to represent the Golden family and their Lord.

Marriage—Passing the Heritage _____

The marriage of our (Otis) two older children provided a perfect setting for the passing of the heritage that Gail and I were handed from our parents. The ceremonies were moving. The impact on the two couples as well as some in the audience was eternal. During each ceremony, the grandparents moved to the altar and told how they had kept the heritage safe. They identified what the heritage embraced in content and explained how they had handed it off to Gail and me.

Then Becky's grandfather said, "Justin and Becky, your grandma and I have prayed for this moment. The heritage we handed your mother and father, they now give to you." His hand came out of his coat pocket revealing some coins. He placed them on the altar. "Here is the cost of two phone calls. One for each of you. When troubles come, and they always do, use these to call, day or night. They are a part of the heritage you received from us. We will always be there for you, Becky. And we will always be there for you, Justin."[2]

In such a ceremony, the parents of the couple step forward and symbolically hand the baton to the next generation. In our children's wedding, this meant words of explanation of how the heritage was held by us for them. We explained that the responsibility for handing it to the next generation was in their hands. They were then asked to keep it safe for generations yet to be born. I read the passage in Psalms that illustrates this principle.

> *He decreed statutes for Jacob and established the law in Israel,*
> *which he commanded our forefathers to teach their children, so*
> *the next generation would know them,* even the children yet
> to be born, *and they in turn would tell their children. Then*
> *they would put their trust in God* (Ps. 78:5-7).

Most ministers have a direction they want a wedding ceremony to take. Handing off the heritage will not interfere with the sequence of any preplanned effort. During the premarital counseling sessions, this subject can be addressed and integrated with the rest of the wedding protocol. Those who have added this to the ceremony testify to the depth of the impression it has made on their families, connecting the distant past to the future.

⁂ *Chapter 12* ⁂

The Refuge of Traditions

⤸⤺⤸⤺

In 1989, an earthquake hit Armenia. Over thirty thousand people were killed in a matter of minutes. Afterward, a father left his house and rushed to the school where he knew his son had been at the time of the quake. He found the building had been leveled and remembered the promise he had once made to his son: "No matter what, I'll always be there for you!" But as he looked at the pile of debris, the father felt hopeless. Tears filled his eyes. What could he possibly do? Still, he kept thinking about the commitment he had made.

Suddenly, he remembered where his son's classroom was, in the back right corner of the building. He rushed to the spot and started digging through the rubble with his hands. Other heartbroken parents arrived. They were crying and saying, "My son!" "My daughter!" Some tried to pull him away from the debris, saying, "It's too late! They're dead! You can't help. Go home! Face reality, there is nothing you can do! You are just going to make things worse!"

The father responded, "Won't you help me?" and continued

to dig for his son, moving one stone at a time. A fire chief tried to pull him away, telling him fires were breaking out and explosions were happening all around them. But the Armenian father responded, "Won't you help me?" The police told him he was endangering others and should go home, but again he replied, "Won't you help me?" and he proceeded alone.

The father dug for eight hours . . . twelve hours . . . thirty-six hours. Then, in the fortieth hour, he pulled back a boulder and heard his son's voice. He screamed his son's name, "ARMAND!"

"Dad! It's me. Dad! I told the other kids not to worry. I told them that if you were alive, you'd save me and when you saved me, they'd be saved. You did it, Dad!"

When the building collapsed, it had made a wedge like a triangle, and saved the lives of thirteen other children still alive with Armand.

Armand's father said, "Come on out, boy!"

"No, Dad! Let the other kids out first. No matter what, I know you'll be there for me!"[1]

As we seek to use our family traditions to pass on stories, beliefs, and customs to our children, the goal is to reinforce a strong sense of identity and an abiding faith in God. We want the bond to be reinforced with an unshakable trust, the kind that prompts our child to say, "No matter what, I know you will be there for me!"

> . . . . .
> ## *Masterpiece Calendar*
> For the New Year, we make a calendar featuring the kids' twelve best seasonal drawings from the year before. We proudly display the calendar and use it to schedule family events, appointments, and traditions!
> *Lori Davis, Wheaton, IL*
> . . . .

A Worthwhile Inheritance _____

How can we pass on this kind of inheritance to our children? What can we do to provide our children with a strong family connection and a heart for God? What steps should we take to build a foundation of trust in our relationships with our children? Scripture gives us the answers to these questions.

> *He who fears the Lord has a secure fortress, and for his children it will be a refuge* (Prov. 14:26).

Our respect and obedience to the Lord provides a secure fortress for our children. They are protected by our faith. It is a shield against the destructive elements of our culture. A godly faith is a source of protection and direction, for parents and their children. One of the best things we can pass on to our children is an example of a vibrant, growing faith. It will be a refuge for our children. They don't have to take on life by themselves. They learn they can trust God to walk with them on life's journey. We prepare our children for life when we help them depend on that which will outlive us: God and His Word.

Our aim in this book has been to help you pass on a godly heritage through the use of family traditions. Traditions that are rooted in faith provide children with a shelter against the prevailing gusts that seek to rob them of their inheritance. God's last word in the Old Testament is stern, but it offers us this choice.

> *See, I will send you the prophet Elijah before that great and dreadful day of the Lord comes. He will turn the hearts of the fathers to their children, and the hearts of the children to their fathers; or else I will come and strike the land with a curse* (Mal. 4:5-6).

We have two choices: to pass on lunacy—the dysfunction and result of sin passed on to us, or legacy—an emotional, spiritual, and social inheritance. Your heart is *toward* your children.

You want to develop meaningful traditions that strengthen your family's faith and provide a refuge, an important theme in Scripture and God's last word in the Old Testament. After God declares this message, four hundred years of silence pass. Talk about a dramatic pause! But the next time God speaks, His first word in the New Testament is again about generational blessing. In Matthew we read the genealogy of Christ through the line of David. The world was blessed. We can pass on blessing or cursing from generation to generation. If our hearts are *toward* our children and the Lord, we will experience His blessing. Traditions set up meaningful exchanges between parent and child, from heart to heart.

> .....
>
> ## *Toddler Dedication*
>
> Due to a family trauma, we didn't get around to dedicating our son Mark in his infant years; we did put together a dedication for him when he was three. My advice is make sure you dedicate your kids before they can talk. When the pastor asked Mark to sing "Jesus Loves Me," Mark said, "No, I'd rather sing the Chuck E. Cheese theme song."
>
> Lori Davis, Wheaton, IL
>
> ....

You Look Just like Your Father _____

The Bible is God's family photo album. It contains snapshots of His kids and stories about them. Some of His children did well and others didn't. Scripture is realistic—not sugarcoated. His children were made in His image and are being shaped into His likeness through the molds of testing and life-transforming faith. There is a family likeness!

Virelle Kidder, mother of four grown children, writes about looking like our Heavenly Father:

> God's heart yearns for His children to become image-bearers,
> "blameless and pure, children of God without fault in a

crooked and depraved generation, in which you shine like stars in the universe as you hold out the word of life" (Phil. 2:15-16). *The great legacy of the Christian home is bearing the family likeness of Christ to the next generation. . . . When we warm our Heavenly Father's heart by faithfully bearing His image and releasing children who do the same, we share in the same heritage as David. This I believe, is our most important purpose in parenting.*[2]

What can you do to develop Christlike character in your children? All of the traditions outlined in this book will help.

A Starting Place

Perhaps you are frustrated because you like all of the ideas in this book, but aren't sure where to start. Let us make a simple suggestion: *Start in the dining room.*

Make it simple. This, you can do.

Eat together.

It may surprise you, but many families don't do that! The disappearing dinner hour is a telltale sign of disintegrating families. According to the American Psychological Society,

a team of psychologists announced the results of a dinnertime study. They categorized 527 teenagers as either well adjusted or not, then looked at the number of times they had dinner at home with their families. The "well adjusted" teens ate with their families five times a week. This group was less likely to do drugs or be depressed, more motivated at school, and had better peer relationships. The teens labeled as "not well adjusted" ate with their families three or fewer days a week. . . . Tom Olkowski, a family practice psychologist, believes that the family dinner hour is dying as a tradition and finds many of the families he sees in his private practice don't have it as an element in their lives. He says, "These small traditions provide a closeness and a sense of security and unity for children.

There's a comfort in the predictability of a routine."[3]

For our family (Tim), routine means Tuesday Taco Night and Friday Pizza Night. We have foods the kids enjoy. We look forward to being together and enjoying our favorite food. Now that our children are teenagers, they help out with the cooking or ordering! Some of our best conversations have been over delivered pizza!

A Tradition Planner _____

Congratulations! You have almost completed the book! Now before you rush out and tell all your friends what a great, life-changing experience it was, let's get practical. Let's design a tradition that you will actually use with your family. Look back through the book and review ideas that you could use with this Tradition Planner. Use the planner to design a special holiday tradition or a rite of passage tradition. Use the following sample planner to develop a customized tradition for your family. You'll find blank Tradition Planners on page 208 to copy and use.

Tradition Planner

Name of Family: Morgan   Date: June 7
Scripture: 1 Thes. 2:11-12

Goal: We will balance rules and relationships.
Definition: Traditions—*the practice of handing down stories, beliefs, and customs from one generation to another in order to establish and reinforce a strong sense of identity.*

1. What stories, beliefs, or customs might help develop a fun and meaningful tradition? When Dad was a teenager and took his father's car without asking and got in an accident. God provides the perfect balance between rules and relationships. We want our children to understand grace. We emphasize asking forgiveness when one family member has wronged another.

2. How has a previous generation passed on this belief or value? How important was it to them? Grandma would always
warn us not to let a "root of bitterness get started because it would quickly sprout into a tree." She also said, "Some folks start to bend over because they are carrying a load of unforgiveness." My father taught me to reconcile when I had fights with my schoolmates. After a bloody nose and a torn shirt in third grade, I became a best friend with my opponent thanks to my father's admonishment.

3. Brainstorm a few ways you could model or teach this belief/value to your children: Have the older children develop their own consequences—positive and negative for their behaviors. Study each child to determine his/her love language and speak it daily. Schedule a one-on-one time with each child every two weeks. Play together. Do something that gets you both laughing.

4. Choose one of the ideas listed above:
Idea, Value, or Belief
Play together, to strengthen our relationship

5. What will your new tradition be?
Since John likes basketball, Dad will practice with him on the driveway once during the week after work and once during the weekend.

6. What do you hope to accomplish with this new tradition?
To reinforce the relationship by playing together and sharing something we both enjoy.

7. What resources do you need?
Basketball, thirty minutes each session.

It's Never Too Early or Too Late _____

Whether you are single, engaged, expecting, divorced, a blended family, or have one child or six, it's never too early or too late to get started developing meaningful family traditions. Perhaps you have read this book thinking, *These are great ideas, but they are for somebody else. My family missed it. My kids are too old to start family traditions.* We have good news for you: you can use family traditions to pass on a heritage even if your children are teenagers, young adults, or have children of their own!

God doesn't operate with the same clock as we do. He is not restricted by time. He deals with eternity. By cooperating with Him, we can make up for lost time, and ask Him to help us initiate traditions that will have an impact.

You can design traditions that will impact generations to come by simply using stories, customs, and events to pass on what is important. It will take some effort, and you may not do it perfectly, but that's okay. It doesn't need to be perfect. Besides, since when are families *perfect?* Families, by design, are a little messy; they don't always follow formulas that fit into neat, tidy boxes. All the more reason why you should get started *experimenting* with family traditions. We use the word intentionally—*experiment.* No, you don't have to put on

> *Family Pizza Night*
> On Fridays we order pizza, get a family-oriented video, and let the kids stay up late, usually talking with us after the movie. We end the evening with prayer.
> *Mark DeVries, Nashville, TN*

a white lab coat and feed your children pellets! Just allow yourself what any scientist does—the opportunity for trial and error. If something doesn't work, try another approach.

You may have inherited a "heart of stone" from your parents, but you don't have to pass it on. God is in the renewal business. He wants to do a complete makeover on your heart. Then He wants you to turn your heart toward your children. With your renewed and focused heart, you will be able to pass on a godly heritage using traditions.

> *I will give you a new heart and put a new spirit in you; I will remove from you your heart of stone and give you a heart of flesh* (Ezek. 36:26).

Tom felt alienated from his father. On Fathers' Day he heard a sermon about honoring fathers. He was convicted of his bitterness and the chasm it created. He asked God for a change of heart. "My heart was cold toward my dad; I just didn't care," he said. "I was distancing myself because of the pain. But God helped me see Dad in a new light—with compassion and understanding. I decided to give it a try. I called him and asked if we could get together. He was shocked, but agreed. I took him out for dinner and asked his forgiveness. I asked him if we could have a fresh start. He agreed, and with tears in his eyes, he said, "Tommy, you remember when we used to play baseball and I would pitch? Sometimes when you would strike out, you would plead, 'Daddy, let me have a *do-over.'* Son, I would be glad to let you have a do-over."

> · · · · ·
> ## TV Angel
> On Sundays we gather close
> and watch *Touched by an Angel.*
> The dishes can wait until the
> show is over!
> Irene Sutherland, Widefield, CO
> · · · · ·

The Story of a Hat

I (Otis) never met the man, I only heard about him. His name was Jake. Everyone who had encountered him testified that he had an uncommon common sense. He had a set of values he lived by and all the answers to problems he confronted were measured against those values. Maybe there was a time or two he wavered, they said, but no one can remember. Even through the hard times, he never questioned his values. He learned them from his father and taught them to his own children. His son, Drew, recalled the time his dad went broke.

"Times were hard and everyone was struggling," Drew said with a defensive tone in his voice. "Dad would just sit in his favorite chair and stare out the window. Owing and not being able to pay went against all he believed."

A drought ravaged Jake's crops and soon he found himself in bankruptcy. His creditors understood and cut him slack. But Jake's debt seemed insurmountable. "I saw him rise out of his easy chair," Drew said, "walk over to the fireplace mantle, and pick up a weathered, broad-rimmed western hat. It was one of the items Dad owned from his late father's estate. The hat had a big 'G' embroidered on the front. It stood for Granville, Grandpa's name. The hat displayed sweat rings, dirt, a little grease, and a whole lot of wear. Others in the family were going to toss the hat, but Dad wanted to keep it. I asked him later what he was doing. He told me whenever he put on the hat, he tried to remember how Grandpa would solve this problem. It helped him to remember Grandpa's values. Nothing mystical. It just helped him make right decisions."

Eight years ago, Jake died. Before he left, all his debtors were paid, including interest.

A mutual friend told me the other day that Drew was having difficulty in his marriage. The friend decided to drive by and encourage him, maybe just be there to talk. He said Drew answered the door. He was wearing the old hat with the "G" embroidered on the front.

. . . . .

Family Liturgy

Our routine for family altar (done several times a week) is to begin in unison with the ancient Christian refrain, "Christ has died, Christ is risen, Christ will come again." Then we read a short passage. We say together, "This is the Word of the Lord; thanks be to God," and sing a hymn or contemporary song. Our goal is to help grow an appreciation for our children's individual connection to the church through the centuries. We want to instill a habit of spirituality in our children.

Susan Miller, Colorado Springs, CO

. . . .

Grandpa's hat held no monetary value. But it possessed tradition, and just like Jake, Drew found refuge in it. The hat was a monument to the values passed to him from previous generations.

Pass It On

The summer I (Tim) turned fourteen, I went to South Dakota to stay with my mother's parents, Grandpa and Grandma Cleveland. My grandfather managed Camp Judson, nestled in the Black Hills. Grandpa Cleveland had many habits, rituals, and traditions. His habits included rising early, reading his well-worn Bible at the breakfast table, working hard ("you aren't working if you aren't sweating"), and always sharpening a tool before he used it ("the right tool for the job makes it easy, a sharp tool makes it easier yet"). His nightly ritual was to kick off his black Wellington slip-on boots, prop his feet up, and enjoy a huge bowl of homemade ice cream—usually peach. It didn't matter who was at the house or what the day brought—it always brought ice cream at the end.

In his honor, I have maintained the nightly ritual.

But it wasn't my grandfather's habits or rituals that made the most impact—it was his traditions: *the beliefs and customs that he talked about and passed on.* One of his traditions was storytelling. He loved to swap stories with the campers and staff. Before Camp Judson, he had spent many years as a circuit-riding preacher, riding horses, then later, driving cars, to preach from church to church on Sundays. He was paid whatever was contributed in that Sunday's offering; with it he raised a large family. If you talk to people who knew him, they may not mention his sermons, but they are likely to retell one of his stories about farming, hunting, the outdoors, and fishing—many of them true! But Grandpa almost always naturally wove in a point, a moral, a virtue, or a biblical principle.

This is what we have tried to do in this book—tell the story of traditions.

Will you pass it on to others?

Traditions are a way of being there after you are gone. They are a means to pass on a godly heritage. By using traditions, you influence your children, even when you aren't with them.

If we use traditions to pass on a heritage, our children will have the stability and faith they need to take on life's challenges. They will feel our support and our emotional presence. When they face trauma, like Armand, the boy trapped in the rubble of the earthquake, they will be able to say, "I knew you would be there for me!"

Appendix
Monument Planner[1]

Event: Date/age:

Name of child:

Purpose of event:

Scriptural purpose:

Theme and Scripture:

Symbols and gifts: What they represent:

People to include in planning: What each will do:

People to invite:

Schedule:

Budget:

Monument Planner

Event: Date/age:

Name of child:

Purpose of event:

Scriptural purpose:

Theme and Scripture:

Symbols and gifts: What they represent:

People to include in planning: What each will do:

People to invite:

Schedule:

Budget:

Monument Planner

Event: Date/age:

Name of child:

Purpose of event:

Scriptural purpose:

Theme and Scripture:

Symbols and gifts: What they represent:

People to include in planning: What each will do:

People to invite:

Schedule:

Budget:

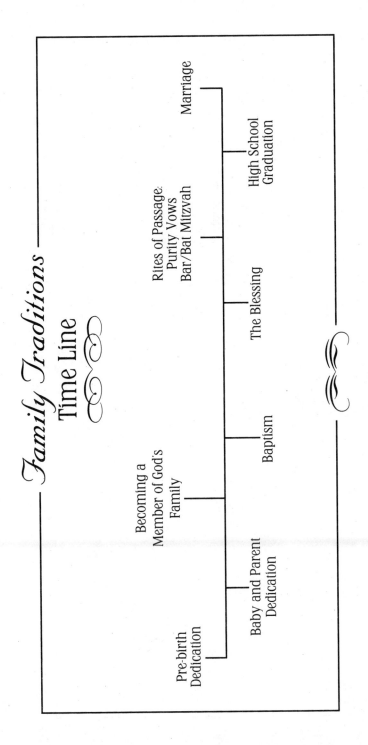

Family Traditions
Time Line

Pre-birth Dedication

Baby and Parent Dedication

Becoming a Member of God's Family

Baptism

The Blessing

Rites of Passage:
Purity Vows
Bar/Bat Mitzvah

High School Graduation

Marriage

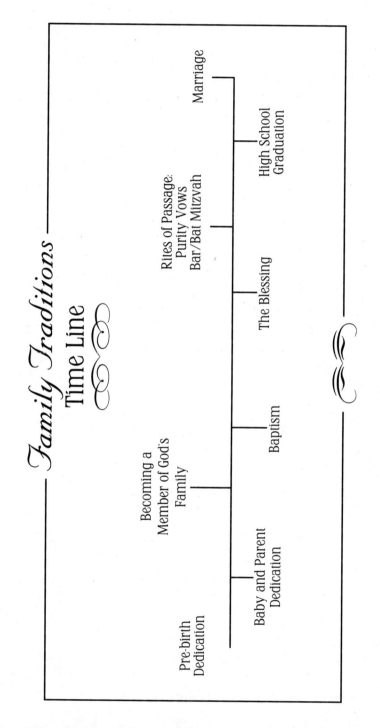

Family Traditions
Time Line

Pre-birth Dedication

Baby and Parent Dedication

Becoming a Member of God's Family

Baptism

The Blessing

Rites of Passage:
Purity Vows
Bar/Bat Mitzvah

High School Graduation

Marriage

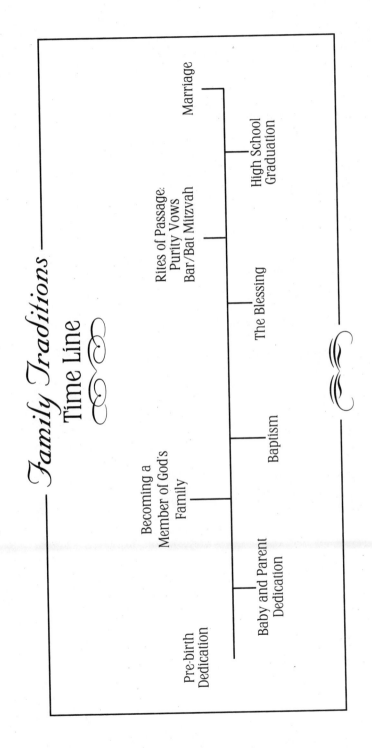

Family Traditions
Time Line

Pre-birth Dedication

Baby and Parent Dedication

Becoming a Member of God's Family

Baptism

The Blessing

Rites of Passage: Purity Vows Bar/Bat Mitzvah

High School Graduation

Marriage

Event

Why do we celebrate this event?

What Scripture is important?

Who should be involved in planning this event?

Is there a theme or atmosphere to capture?

How much will the tradition event vary from individual to individual?

Event

Why do we celebrate this event?

What Scripture is important?

Who should be involved in planning this event?

Is there a theme or atmosphere to capture?

How much will the tradition event vary from individual to individual?

Event

Why do we celebrate this event?

What Scripture is important?

Who should be involved in planning this event?

Is there a theme or atmosphere to capture?

How much will the tradition event vary from individual to individual?

Target:
A Mature and Prepared Young Adult

The four skill areas my children need to begin life on their own.

To make wise decisions:

To possess character:

To have vision and purpose:

To have and use life skills:

Target:
A Mature and Prepared Young Adult

The four skill areas my children need to begin life on their own.

To make wise decisions:

To possess character:

To have vision and purpose:

To have and use life skills:

Target:
A Mature and Prepared Young Adult

The four skill areas my children need to begin life on their own.

To make wise decisions:

To possess character:

To have vision and purpose:

To have and use life skills:

Tradition Planner

Name of Family: Date:
Scripture:
Goal:

Definition: Traditions—*the practice of handing down stories, beliefs, and customs from one generation to another in order to establish and reinforce a strong sense of identity.*

1. What stories, beliefs, or customs might help develop a fun and meaningful tradition?

2. How has a previous generation passed on this belief or value? How important was it to them?

3. Brainstorm a few ways you could model or teach this belief/value to your children:

4. Choose one of the ideas listed above:
Idea, Value, or Belief

5. What will your new tradition be?

6. What do you hope to accomplish with this new tradition?

7. What resources do you need?

Tradition Planner

Name of Family: Date:
Scripture:
Goal:

Definition: Traditions—*the practice of handing down stories, beliefs, and customs from one generation to another in order to establish and reinforce a strong sense of identity.*

1. What stories, beliefs, or customs might help develop a fun and meaningful tradition?

2. How has a previous generation passed on this belief or value? How important was it to them?

3. Brainstorm a few ways you could model or teach this belief/value to your children:

4. Choose one of the ideas listed above:
Idea, Value, or Belief

5. What will your new tradition be?

6. What do you hope to accomplish with this new tradition?

7. What resources do you need?

Tradition Planner

Name of Family: Date:
Scripture:
Goal:

Definition: Traditions—*the practice of handing down stories, beliefs, and customs from one generation to another in order to establish and reinforce a strong sense of identity.*

1. What stories, beliefs, or customs might help develop a fun and meaningful tradition?

2. How has a previous generation passed on this belief or value? How important was it to them?

3. Brainstorm a few ways you could model or teach this belief/value to your children:

4. Choose one of the ideas listed above:
Idea, Value, or Belief

5. What will your new tradition be?

6. What do you hope to accomplish with this new tradition?

7. What resources do you need?

Traditions Index

Dedications

Easter

Family Time

Journals

Meals

St. Patrick's Day

Valentine's Day

&ndnotes

Chapter 1

1 Adapted from J. Otis Ledbetter and Kurt Bruner, *The Heritage* (Colorado Springs, CO: Chariot Victor Publishing, 1996) 103.

Chapter 2

1 Wes Haystead, *The 3,000 -Year-Old Guide To Parenting* (Ventura, CA: Regal, 1991) 17.

2 J. Otis and Gail Ledbetter, *Family Fragrance,* (Colorado Springs, CO: Chariot Victor, 1998) 27-28.

3 Leo Trepp, *The Complete Book of Jewish Observance, A Practical Manual for the Modern Jew* (N.Y.: Simon & Schuster, 1980) xiii.

4 Edith Schaeffer, *Christianity Is Jewish* (Wheaton, IL: Tyndale, 1975) 23.

Chapter 3

1 Schaeffer, *Christianity Is Jewish* , 87-88.

2 David R. Veerman, *Ozzie & Harriet Had a Scriptwriter* (Wheaton, IL: Tyndale, 1996) 78.

Chapter 4

1 Schaeffer, *Christianity Is Jewish,* 60.

2 Trepp, *The Complete Book of Jewish Observance.*

Chapter 5

1 Tim Kimmel, *Raising Kids Who Turn Out Right* (Sisters, OR: Multnomah, 1993) 137.

2 Haystead, *The 3,000-Year-Old Guide to Parenting,* 60.

3 Lawrence O. Richards, *Expository Dictionary of Bible Words* (Grand Rapids, MI: Zondervan, 1985) 597.

4 Dean and Grace Merrill, *Together At Home* (Colorado Springs, CO: Focus on the Family, 1988) 9.

Chapter 6

1 Ceil and Moishe Rosen, *Christ in the Passover*, (Chicago, IL: Moody, 1978) 9.
2 Ibid. 10.
3 Trepp, *The Complete Book of Jewish Observance*, 3.
4 Ibid. 44
5 Ibid. 103
6 Ibid. 123

Chapter 7

1 Tim Smith, *The Relaxed Parent—Helping Your Kids Do More as You Do Less* (Chicago: Northfield, 1996), 205.
2 Veerman, *Ozzie and Harriet Had a Scriptwriter*, 78.
3 Walt Mueller, *Understanding Today's Youth Culture* (Wheaton , IL: Tyndale, 1994) 337.
4 Gary Chapman and Ross Campbell, M.D., *The Five Love Languages of Children* (Chicago: Northfield, 199?)
5 Ledbetter and Bruner, *The Heritage* , 176.
6 Douglas S. Barasch, "Religion and Spirituality," *Family Life*, Winter 1998, (N.Y.: Hachette Filipacchi Magazines) 90.
7 Ibid. 91 adapted.
8 Ledbetter and Bruner, *The Heritage*, 181.
9 Barasch, , "Religion and Spirituality," 94.

Chapter 8

1 Becky Tirabassi, "A House Built On Stone," *Focus on the Family*, Feb. 1998, (Colorado Springs, CO: Focus on the Family) 2.
2 Kimmel, *Raising Kids Who Turn Out Right*, 14.
3 Ibid. 36.
4 Haystead, *The 3,000 Year-Old Guide to Parenting*, 92.
5 Kimmel, *Raising Kids Who Turn Out Right*, 37.

Chapter 9

1 John and Carol Dettoni, *Parenting Before & After Work* (Wheaton, IL: Victor, 1992) 64.
2 Tim Smith, adapted, *Almost Cool—You Can Figure Out How to Parent Your Teen* (Chicago: Moody, 1997) 149.
3 Dettoni, *Parenting Before & After Work* , 113 (brackets added).
4 Veerman, *Ozzie and Harriet Had a Scriptwriter*, 79

5 Merton and Irene Strommen, *Five Cries of Parents* (San Francisco: Harper and Row, 1985) 94-95.

Chapter 10

1 C.S. Lewis, "Pindar Sang," *Poems*, 1949, 16.
2 Smith, adapted, *Almost Cool*, 106-107.
3 Smith, adapted, *Letters to Nicole*, 46-47.

Chapter 11

1 Smith, *Almost Cool*, 101-102.
2 Ledbetter and Bruner, *The Heritage*, 21.

Chapter 12

1 Jim Burns and Greg McKinnon, *Illustrations, Stories and Quotes* (Ventura, CA: Gospel Light, 1997) 35-36.
2 Virelle Kidder, *Loving, Launching and Letting Go—Preparing Your Nearly-Grown Children for Adulthood* (Nashville, TN: Broadman and Holman, 1995) 160-161.
3 Linda DuVal, "Disappearing Dinner Hour," *The Sunday Oregonian*, March 29, 1998.

Appendix

1 All charts and planners in *Family Traditions* may be copied for use in your family. © 1998 by J. Otis Ledbetter and Tim Smith. Used by permission.

If you liked this book from
Chariot Victor Publishing,
check out this great title . . .

The authors bring together years of experience to create 12
fun-filled sessions on holidays throughout the year, from
Easter and Valentine's Day to Thanksgiving and Christmas.
The goal is for families to spend time with their children on a
regular basis to stimulate spiritual growth.

Holiday Family Nights
by Jim Weidman & Kurt Bruner & Ron Wilson
ISBN: 1-56476-737-X

and this great title . . .

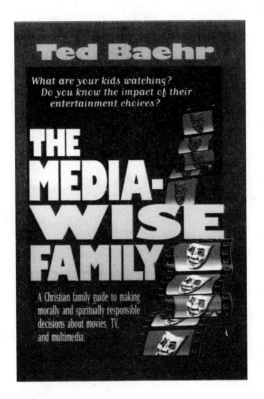

Media-Wise examines how people use media,
especially TV and movies, how children learn, and
the media's effect on them. Includes many
practical ways to teach children to be discerning
in media use.

The Media-Wise Family
by by Ted Baehr
ISBN: 0-78140-301-4

. . . and this great title.

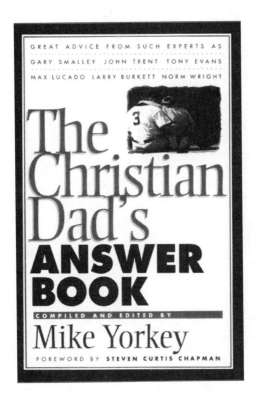

This book compiles the best information from the leading
Christian experts in the perfect question-and-answer format.
Besides dad-specific themes, it covers a variety of other topics
such as work, finances, and difficult problems.

The Christian Dad's Answer Book
by Mike Yorkey
ISBN: 1-56476-677-2